Change in Myanmar

Change in Myanmar

Edited by

Rajiv K. Bhatia

Vijay Sakhuja

Vikash Ranjan

SHIPRA

INDIAN COUNCIL OF WORLD AFFAIRS

This book is based on the proceedings of a joint conference 'Change in Myanmar: Impact on India-Myanmar Relations' held on 6 March 2013 at Yangon, organized by the Indian Council of World Affairs (ICWA), New Delhi; Embassy of India, Yangon; and Myanmar Institute of Strategic and International Studies (MISIS), Yangon. The text has therefore been edited and suitably modified for the readers. The views expressed in this volume are of individual contributors and do not represent the viewpoint of the editors or the Council.

Rs. 750; US$ 37.50

ISBN: 978-81-7541-758-8

First Published in India in 2014

Change in Myanmar

Published by:
SHIPRA PUBLICATIONS
H.O.: LG 18-19, Pankaj Central Market, Patparganj,
I.P. Ext., Delhi-110092, Tel: 91-11-2223 5152, 2223 6152
Br.Off.: 4617/18, Ansari Road, Darya Ganj,
New Delhi-110002, Tel: 9650028065, 9810522367
E-mail: info@shiprapublication.com
www.shiprapublication.com

Foreword

India's Myanmar policy is guided by national interest and geostrategic significance. This edited book, based on an important seminar on 'Change in Myanmar: Impact on India-Myanmar Relations', has been brought out with the objective of deepening and strengthening India-Myanmar relations by disseminating knowledge about the relationship to the wider audience.

The visit of ICWA-sponsored delegation in March 2013 demonstrated the commitment of India's leading Track II institutions to further study, research and evaluate knowledge about 'the new Myanmar' in the backdrop of historic internal developments as well as important recent trends in the bilateral, regional and international context. The seminar reflected a new bond of cooperation between the Myanmar Institute of Strategic and International Studies (MISIS) and the Indian Council of World Affairs (ICWA), resulting from the MoU signed between the two institutions during the Indian Prime Minister's visit to Myanmar in May 2012. The delegation consisted of well-known Myanmar scholars from the Institute of Defence Studies and Analyses (IDSA)—another MoU partner of MISIS, Indian Council for Research on International Economic Relations (ICRIER), Observer Research Foundation (ORF), Research and Information System for Developing Countries (RIS) and Delhi University, besides ICWA. Ambassador Shyam Saran, former foreign secretary, former special envoy of the Prime Minster, former ambassador to Myanmar, and the present Chairman of RIS, was a distinguished delegate from the Indian side. The seminar was hosted by MISIS, the premier Myanmar institution on foreign policy matters. Its Chairman, Ambassador Nyunt Maung Shein, visited India early in 2013 to participate in ICWA flagship conference on India-ASEAN relations, Delhi Dialogue V. ICWA had also the privilege to host a lecture by HE U Wunna Maung Lwin, Foreign Minister of Myanmar, in January 2012.

In June 2011, when I visited Myanmar at the invitation of MISIS, to participate in an international seminar entitled 'Myanmar and the International Community—the Way Forward' Myanmar was at a critical stage in the evolution of reform process. President Thein Sein had announced his reform agenda through his 30 March, 2011 inaugural speech before the Parliament, but the reconciliation between the Government and NLD was yet to happen. (It followed the meeting between Daw Aung San Suu Kyi and the President in August 2011.) On return from the Yangon seminar, I wrote in an Op-ed of a prestigious national daily, stating

> I returned with a clear impression that Myanmar is passing through a complex transition: the old era of the State Peace and Development Council rule has ended and the new era of 'civilian' rule, with all its imperfections, has begun.

Since then, the Government's reform caravan has performed an impressive journey, securing one achievement after another, like, operationalisation of the new Parliament after November 2010 elections, and other democratic institutions established under the 2008 Constitution; release of political prisoners and normalisation of political life; granting of a variety of freedoms to labour, media and civil society; and undertaking of an ambitious programme of economic liberalisation and development. As a result, the country's political and socio-economic landscape has changed substantially. Recognition of this change by Myanmar's international partners has been swift, substantial and somewhat competitive in nature.

However, in spite of these positive trends, Myanmar people—leaders, spokesmen and experts —point out that the country's journey has just begun. Complex challenges such as the ethnic conflict and the imperative need to resolve it through sustained reconciliation, strife in the Rakhine state, constitutional reform, a whole range of governance issues, and the national goal of securing accelerated economic growth, confront the nation.

Managing foreign policy in a fast transforming environment, while taking into consideration the geo-political developments, may be another challenge. In a speech, the US Secretary of State, John Kerry stated: 'There is no longer anything foreign about foreign policy.' He added: 'More than ever before, the decisions that we make from the safety of our shores do not just ripple outward; they also create a current right here in America.' I would only stress that these wise words are applicable to Myanmar and India as much as they apply to the US.

Indian delegates benefitted from the Myanmar side's informed perceptions, which helped us to refine our understanding of various aspects of Myanmar's reform strategy and foreign policy. It goes without saying that, as a reciprocal gesture, the Indian delegation assisted the Myanmar side in comprehending and appreciating various aspects of Indian polity and public policy.

The other significant objective of the seminar was to have an in-depth examination and appraisal of India's multi-faceted relationship with Myanmar. This was undertaken against the larger historical backdrop, even as the two sides focussed on assessing developments in the past two years. It seems that the period that started with President Thein Sein's visit to India in October 2011, witnessed the landmark visit of Prime Minister Manmohan Singh in May 2012, and ended with the Lok Sabha Speaker's visit to Myanmar in February 2013, may be considered as one of the most productive and positive phases in the development of bilateral relations. Clearly, the change in Myanmar, flowing from the emergence of a new national consensus and reconciliation, had beneficial impact on India-Myanmar relations.

While examining new trends in the bilateral relationship and its regional dimensions, a special mention of the Vision Statement issued at the ASEAN-India Commemorative Summit of December 2012, is necessary. Especially, two of its provisions are relevant, namely, (i) ASEAN's appreciation of 'India's commitment to continue the special focus on the CLMV countries that represent a bridge between ASEAN and India' through human resource development and capacity building; and (ii) the joint commitment to enhance connectivity through various measures.

What has been the effect of new bilateral agreements, particularly those concluded during Prime Minister Manmohan Singh's visit to Myanmar as well as before and after that visit? Are there still constraints and impediments in the path of further development of bilateral relations? What can India and Myanmar do differently? Which other areas the two sides need to explore further? Can we suggest new measures and ideas to policy makers? With these questions, the seminar did not simply review past developments, but strove to draw fresh conclusions and craft creative recommendations for future.

The two sides attempted to review the past, evaluate the present, and re-imagine the future. The central challenge for the two delegations was to work together as scholars and produce in due course a set of joint recommendations, with the aim to take this vital relationship to the next higher level, maybe even to a new strategic partnership. This book aims at filling all these gaps and quench the thirst for deeper understanding and stronger friendship between Myanmar and India.

Rajiv K. Bhatia,
Director General,
Indian Council of World Affairs

Prologue

It gives me great pleasure to welcome the ICWA delegation led by Ambassador Rajiv K Bhatia to the MISIS. I am also very much delighted to see Ambassador Shyam Saran in the ICWA delegation. As you all know, both these distinguished Ambassadors had served in Myanmar representing India. So, they are old and true friends of Myanmar. I recall working closely with Ambassador Shyam Saran when I was heading the Political Department as the Director General.

Last year, during the historic visit of Prime Minister Manmohan Singh to Myanmar, MISIS signed the MoU with ICWA to further strengthen the cooperation between the two institutions. The presence of the ICWA delegation in Myanmar for the first time to hold an exchange of views between the scholars and experts from the two sides is a step in that direction.

I must underline the fact that we are holding this first dialogue between the MISIS and ICWA at a very important juncture, i.e., coinciding with the assumption of the Chair of ASEAN by Myanmar next year at which time the final preparations must be made for the realization of the ASEAN Economic Community in 2015. An issue such as connectivity is an important aspect of the ASEAN Community. In this respect, Myanmar will play a very important role in connecting India with the rest of ASEAN. I am quite sure, we will touch on the connectivity issue in our discussions.

The ICWA has a history of seventy years, while MISIS is only 20 years old. Therefore, it is quite natural that ICWA has a wealth of experience and expertise in many areas of study and in various fields. Myanmar ISIS stands to gain from ICWA's experience and knowledge. We look forward to exchange of views in the four sessions: Myanmar's reform process, bilateral political relations, defence and security cooperation, and economic and technical cooperation.

We expect recommendations to emerge from these discussions, which will be jointly prepared as a report and submitted to the respective policy makers as inputs from the Track II institutions of Myanmar and India. I wish all the participants every success in the deliberations.

Ambassador Nyunt Maung Shein
Chairman, Myanmar Institute of Strategic and International Studies

Perspective

India and Myanmar have enjoyed historical, ethnic, cultural, and religious ties. India's relations with Myanmar are guided by New Delhi's 'Look East Policy', which has served as an important tool of its foreign policy. Myanmar has taken a number of positive steps to engage the country with regional and global powers for the growth and development of the country. It has the potential to become a convenient transit route for India's growing trade relations with South-east Asia. Besides ASEAN, India and Myanmar are also cooperating at sub-regional levels, like Mekong Ganga cooperation (MGC), BCIM, and BIMSTEC. Myanmar is also an observer in SAARC. The international community desires Myanmar to democratize, and seeks to ensure that a political transition, when it occurs in Myanmar, is as smooth as possible.

There was a perceived apprehension in Myanmar of the danger of being caught in the crossfire between India and China. India seeks peaceful cooperation with China, both bilaterally and regionally, as it favours a multi-polar world and a multi-polar Asia. India is not in competition with China just as it is not in the interest of any Southeast Asian country to be in competition with China. As a developing country, India seeks peaceful environment and desists from confrontation with any country. India's trade with China is on the upswing. As such, China could be a positive factor in the development of the new world order. India seeks balanced security architecture (and activities under the ADMM Plus are welcome), although it is apprehensive of unilateral assertion of power. These are sensitive issues and there is a need for regular dialogue on them. ASEAN can serve as a platform for reconciliation in the region. Even the Vision 2020 document issued after the New Delhi-ASEAN Commemorative Summit in 2012 underlined the centrality of ASEAN.

The Government of India is actively involved in over a dozen projects in Myanmar, both in infrastructural and non-infrastructural areas. These include up-gradation and resurfacing of the 160 km. long Tamu-Kalewa-Kalemyo road; construction and up-gradation of the Rhi-Tiddim Road in Myanmar; the Kaladan Multimodal Transport Project etc.

RIS is conducting a study for the Ministry of External Affairs on economic and technical cooperation with Myanmar. It will be useful to explore if Myanmar's SEZ concept could apply to India's Northeast border (Manipur's Moreh-Tamu and in Mizoram) as well. India can offer to establish "development corridors" along various infrastructural project routes, with backward and forward linkages, which would be beneficial in bringing growth in both countries.

With these few words, I would like to thank both the Indian Council of World Affairs and Myanmar Institute of Strategic and International Studies for co-hosting this timely seminar on a very important subject.

Ambassador Shyam Saran

Chairman,
Research and Information System for Developing Countries
and former Foreign Secretary

Message

It is a great honour and privilege to welcome two distinguished and senior Indian diplomats, who have both represented India in Myanmar at the highest diplomatic position and contributed immensely in strengthening the age old ties that bind the two countries.

I also wish to take this opportunity to congratulate the two think tanks, Indian Council of World Affairs and Myanmar Institute of Strategic and International Studies, who have come together in organizing this seminar on the topical issue, "Change In Myanmar: Impact on India-Myanmar relations". It is heartening that the two premiere think tanks from the two countries have implemented the spirit of the Memorandum of Understanding signed last year during the visit of Indian Prime Minister, Dr. Manmohan Singh.

India and Myanmar enjoy deep-rooted and multifaceted relations for centuries, enabled by common geography, history, and cultural roots that they share. These close, friendly and good neighbourly relations have been strengthened further through exchange of high level visits in recent times.

Myanmar is perfectly situated to play the critical role of an economic bridge between India and ASEAN. Myanmar is the key to success of India's Look East Policy", a policy which is aimed at strengthening India's relations with all ASEAN member states.

India sees Myanmar as a natural partner and attaches great importance to its relation with Myanmar. This fact came out clear and loud at the annual budget speech of Finance Minister of India, Mr. P. Chidambaram, where he specifically mentioned about Myanmar and enhanced the development cooperation budget for Myanmar while reducing it for others.

During the visit of Prime Minister Dr. Manmohan Singh to Myanmar in May 2012, the two leaders agreed on a vision for the future in the pursuit of the common good—bilaterally, regionally, and globally. They agreed to cooperate in areas such as border area development, transportation, connectivity, agriculture, trade and investment, promotion of friendly exchanges and human resource development. They recognized the need to effectively harness their respective resources for the progress and prosperity of the people of these two countries.

The new government of Myanmar under the leadership of President U Thein Sein has been engaging in serious reform process and has set itself an ambitious agenda of achieving good governance to achieve national political reconciliation and rapid economic development. The new developments in Myanmar have also evoked great interest amongst the international community.

Today, as Myanmar stands at the threshold of political and economic transition to a democratic system and market economy, the two countries' relations are set to move to a higher plane, acquiring new depth and substance. This has also provided India an opportunity to work as equal partners to revive the ancient links and rediscover the immense possibilities of cooperation that exist between the two countries.

India and Myanmar need to work with each other for the prosperity of the two people by promoting openness and exchange of thoughts and ideas. Indian government stands ready to walk the high road of progress with the friendly government of Myanmar.

The Indian missions in Myanmar have been encouraging Indian companies to come and assess opportunities in Myanmar. The response has been overwhelming and today when we are talking about India-Myanmar relations; there are more than 40 Indian businessmen in Nay Pyi Taw from Federation of Indian Chambers of Commerce and Industry (FICCI) and Indian Chamber of Commerce (ICC), Kolkata. I am confident that as the investment climate in Myanmar improves, Indian companies are bound to invest in a variety of sectors for mutual benefit.

There have been increased interactions between both countries at all levels covering the entire gamut of relations. This trend needs to be encouraged and provided right directions. A seminar like this where, think-tanks of the two countries are coming together and exchanging ideas is not only timely, but also apt and topical.

We could not have asked for more in terms of resource persons than what we have today in the Indian delegation. Ambassador Shyam Saran and Ambassador Rajiv Bhatia, former Ambassadors of India to Myanmar, are depositories of India-Myanmar relations and are the main architects, who laid the concrete foundation of the present multi-faceted relations.

I have no doubt in my mind that this seminar will be a massive investment of ideas to India-Myanmar bilateral relations and will provide catalyst and directions for more vibrant relations. With these few words, I would like to wish the seminar a great success.

Sailas Thanggal

Deputy Chief of Mission,

Embassy of India, Yangon

Contents

Introduction

Myanmar has witnessed a number of positive political developments in recent times. It drafted a new Constitution, held a referendum to approve it, organized elections and put in place a new Parliament and government. These changes also encouraged the most staunch opposition leader, Nobel-laureate Ms. Aung San Suu Kyi and her party, the National League for Democracy to join the process.

The reform process currently underway in Myanmar has provided opportunities to the international community to engage with the country and carry the momentum forward. Still, there are some apprehensions regarding the reform process. The US-Myanmar relations have shown signs of rapprochement. The Myanmar President, Mr. Thein Sein and Ms. Aung San Suu Kyi both visited the US, and after his re-election, President Barack Obama also made a historic visit to Nay Pyi Taw enroute to Phnom Penh for the East Asia Summit in 2012. The EU too has lifted sanctions and a number of European countries have engaged with the country through diplomatic and commercial interactions. Likewise, many other regional countries, like Australia, Japan, South Korea and others have started engaging with Myanmar in a big way.

India and Myanmar have shared historical ties of over more than three millennia. The bilateral relations are guided by New Delhi's 'Look East policy', which has served as an important tool of its foreign policy. India's relations with Myanmar are on the upswing after Prime Minister Manmohan Singh made a historic visit to the country in

June 2012. In the economic domain, the bilateral trade has doubled in the last five years and is currently pegged at US$ 1.8 billion. India has enormous stakes in developing good relations with Myanmar for developing its northeast region. It offers a convenient transit route for India's growing trade with Southeast Asia, and also the opportunities to develop its linkages with sub regional groupings, such as BIMSTEC, BCIM, Mekong Ganga cooperation (MGC), etc. Cooperation with Myanmar is also important from the perspective of India's internal security and non-traditional security issues, like energy security. A number of Indian oil and gas companies are engaged in exploration activities in the Bay of Bengal. Likewise, there are opportunities to help Myanmar enhance its food security, improve the standards of living of the people through capacity building, technological exchanges and through other means.

Defence and security cooperation between the two countries is important as Myanmar needs security and stability to promote its reform processes. Anticipating these challenges, India and Myanmar can cooperate in non-traditional security issues, which may arise in the region.

It is hoped that this volume will contribute to a better understanding of India-Myanmar relations.

Vijay Sakhuja
Vikash Ranjan

Section I

Reform Process: Achievements and the Way Forward

1
Reform Process: Achievements and the Way Forward

Udai Bhanu Singh

Myanmar is going through a significant phase in its history when fundamental changes are being effected in its political, economic and social domains in a short span of time—something this writer noticed during an earlier visit to the country.[1]

The opportunities, which arose on earlier occasions in 1990, 2007 or 2008, did not fructify in any meaningful sense (in terms of political reform). The National League for Democracy (NLD) failed to come to power in spite of securing a majority in the May 2010 elections. The 2007 public protests (with the support of Buddhist monks) were suppressed and did not quite parallel events in neighbouring Indonesia, or the Philippines. Neither could the chaos of the cyclone Nargis in May 2008 translate into a victory for democracy. But the State Peace and Development Council (SPDC) presented its own roadmap to democracy and its own vision of a 'discipline-flourishing democracy'. The SPDC has yielded political space to a civil government and the military junta no longer exists in any formal sense, though the military continues to dominate the new political structure. Does the new political structure contain seeds of change or is it designed to block further change? Is this transition meaningful or not? Change was introduced with regional governments being elected consequent to the 2010 elections and the bye-elections, later, saw Aung San Suu Kyi and her party being elected. Would the Constitutional Tribunal move towards greater autonomy? More urgent than a change in the Constitution perhaps is a change in the implementation mechanism and the need for better governance. The military's role in the judicial system has now declined, but there is need to reform the police and root out corruption. As the next general elections are due in 2015 all eyes are on Myanmar to see if political reform is completed by that time or not. And if political reforms remain incomplete, would the next winner carry them forward.

The transformation has gained momentum as the rapid gains have got telescoped in the past two years, and both domestic and external players have participated in this process of transformation. Will the current reforms meet the expectations of its people or those of other interested actors? In any case, after a long period of isolation, it may not be prudent to expect an overnight transformation, as there are institutions that need to be reformed and there needs to be a change in some old ways of functioning.

There is a vast array of literature on the transition theory; starting with Huntington, Diamond, O'Donnell, Schmitter, Lipset and others. The transition paradigm makes the assumption that democratisation occurs sequentially ('opening', 'breakthrough' and 'consolidation' stages). This theory was squarely debunked by Thomas Carothers, who said: "It is time for the democracy-promotion community to discard the transition paradigm". The Transition paradigm's Achilles heel lay in its underestimation of the importance of the underlying conditions in a transitional country, such as its economic level, political history, institutional legacy, ethnic makeup and socio-cultural tradition. The institutions in Myanmar, as we are aware, have been systematically eroded. Here, the writings of Ashley South become relevant. He identifies two approaches for political change in Myanmar: regime reform and regime change. This nuanced approach, which helps deal with grey zone countries, is relevant as the goal of democracy is not being achieved in a linear fashion in Southeast and East Asia.

President Thein Sein's inaugural speech to Parliament on 30 March 2011 outlined the national agenda on the political, economic and social front. He referred to three national causes, which are non-negotiable, i.e. non-disintegration of the Union, non-disintegration of the national solidarity, and perpetuation of sovereignty. He further said that Myanmar needs three types of might to accomplish these national causes: (a) political might (b) economic might and (c) military might. By political might, he meant national unity.[2] He referred to the right of the people (under Chapter XII of the Constitution) to amend the 2008 Constitution. Interestingly, when he spoke of, 'military might', he implicitly asserted the civilian supremacy over the military.

Political Reforms

Political reforms, in accordance with the 'roadmap to democracy' heralded the change in Myanmar. A new Constitution (resulting from the long drawn out deliberations of the National Convention) was put into effect in 2008 after a referendum approved it. Elections (Union and State legislatures) followed thereafter on 7 November 2010.[3] A new Parliament was inaugurated in Naypyitaw on 31 January 2011. Finally, a new Government headed by the President was sworn in on 30 March 2011, which also marked the dissolution of the SPDC. President Thein Sein undertook a reshuffle of ministry officials. Six officials were forced to retire on grounds of either mismanagement or corruption. Forty other officials were transferred to other ministries.[4] A start was made to improve the human rights situation. Myanmar National Human Rights Commission was established on 5 September 2011. As a result, labour unions could now be formed and demonstrations could be authorized. The exiles could return now.

The "fourth estate" or media began to be freed. The government initially freed some areas in the print media like—entertainment, health, children, information technology and sports from pre-publication scrutiny. Later in December 2011, other areas were added, such as business and crime, helping over 200 publications.[5] The pre-publication censorship rules were ended in August 2012 and the state monopoly over newspapers ended on 1 April 2013, with four private newspapers being allowed to publish.[6] The visual media was also freed and the restrictions on online media were also gradually lifted; fewer websites are blocked now. Google Executive Chairman, Eric Shmidt, during his visit to Myanmar, while commending the government on its decision to open up, said that the empowerment that opening of media confers in terms of the ability to communicate is virtually irreversible.[7] Greater access into the country was given to foreign journalists (for instance, they are allowed the coverage of parliament proceedings).

The political prisoners continue to be released by the government. The President announced a pardon in May 2011, which resulted in the release of 20,000 prisoners including political prisoners by June 2011. After a prolonged period of house arrest, Daw Aung San Suu Kyi (DASSK) herself was released on 13 November 2010. This was preceded initially by negotiations with DASSK by the government at the level of Minister Aung Kyi in 2007. Meetings were held between the two in July-August 2011. This was followed by a meeting between DASSK and the President Thein Sein on 19 August 2011. The Political Parties Registration Law was amended in November 2011, allowing the NLD to reregister as a political party.[8] By-elections (April 2012) saw not only the return of the NLD to the national mainstream, but also as the second largest party in the parliament.[9] In so far as personalities have a special place in Myanmar politics, the re-emergence of DASSK began even as the former President Than Shwe slowly went into the background. It is not clear whether he is in a position to pull strings from behind the scene.

The process of political reform in Myanmar has not been all smooth. First on the deficit side (as some weaknesses remain in the Constitution), the special provision of 25 per cent seats in the legislatures for the Military continues to be a point of contention. Parliament announced that a committee of law experts and intellectuals would be formed, which would begin its work to review the Constitution in July 2013.

Military Reforms

Myanmar's Military (SLORC/SPDC), in power for almost fifty years, had taken Indonesia's *dwifungsi* (dual role policy) as a model. As in Indonesia, would the military in Myanmar eventually reconcile itself to a more circumscribed role? The 2008 Constitution provides a dominant role for the armed forces (*tatmadaw*). The President has wide-ranging powers. The Constitution provides special privileges for the *tatmadaw*. In addition, there is an entire chapter devoted to the Defence Services (Chapter VII). These constitutional provisions will probably be amended eventually.

Certain changes have been noticed already. The military's share in the national budget has been marginally reduced this year, which needs to decline further. Second, the role of military in business declined in Indonesia and we may observe similar trends in Myanmar too. Third, DASSK attended the Armed Forces Day ceremony on 27 March 2013 in Naypyitaw for the first time, although she prefers to call it the Resistance Day (against Japanese occupation).[10] Fourth, this reform could be helped along by greater military to military interactions with the militaries of not only India, but also of other countries like the US. All three chiefs of the Indian armed forces have visited Myanmar in the past few months (and earlier as well). The Indian navy too has participated in joint exercises in the Bay of Bengal and it will soon have a Naval Advisor in Indian Embassy in Yangon besides an Army Advisor. Myanmar has already begun participating in the Cobra Gold exercises with the US and could potentially cooperate in further training programmes, given that some of its top military officers have had US military training in the past. Myanmar cooperates with US in Missing in Action (MIA) exercises in the Kachin area to find remains of its servicemen. This would help achieve Myanmar's objective of developing a more professional army.

Social Reforms and the Ethnic Dimension

Perhaps the biggest challenge Myanmar regime faces is the task of national reconciliation among the various ethnic groups. In this respect, its challenge is greater than the challenge Indonesia faced in the post-Suharto era of democratization (where 'unity in diversity' is the proclaimed national motto). Ethnic minorities constitute an important factor in Myanmar's politics. The Burmans make up about two-thirds of the total population, while the Karens, the Shans, the Mons, the Rohingyas, the Chins and Kachins constitute some of the prominent ethnic minorities. President Thein Sein in a speech on 17 August 2011 called for peace talks with the armed factions of each of the minorities. "Any individual and organization in the nation that have different views from the government should not take account of disagreements and we invite them to work with us for common goals in the national interests."[11]

Table 1.1: Ceasefire Agreements concluded with Myanmar's Main Ethnic Minorities

Armed group	*Date of Agreement*
United Wa State Army	September 2011
National Democratic Alliance Army	September 2011
Kloh Htoo baw ("Golden Drum" Group)	November 2011
Shan State Army-South	December 2011
Chin National Front	January 2012
Karen National Union	January 2012
Shan State Army-North	January 2012
New Mon State Party	February 2012
Karen National Liberation Army Peace Council	February 2012
Karenni National Progressive Party	March 2012
Arakan Liberation Party	April 2012

Source: International Crisis Group, "Reform in Myanmar: One Year on".

The deep ethnic animosities in Rakhine and in Kachin states continue to destabilize Myanmar. The commission on Rakhine communal violence submitted its over 100 page report to the President on 22 April 2013. It dealt with the causes of the conflict, solution to the problems that led to the conflict and action points for the government. Earlier, the Human Rights Watch had published a report titled 'All You Can do is Pray".[12] The Rohingya problem continues to pose a challenge to the stability of Rakhine state. In order to control the communal conflict in Meiktila, the government had to call the first special session of the Pyidaungsu Hluttaw to approve the ordinance No. 1/2013 issued for this purpose. Myanmar needs to resolve the Rohingya problem: would that be done by granting them citizenship status or by according them ethnic minority status? Would it come about by reducing the barriers on their movement and absorption in different parts of the country? Many federal solutions to national integrations have been suggested (with their respective strengths and weaknesses) and various models of federalism have been attempted across Europe and Asia. But the model, which would suit Myanmar best, would be the one which takes the local conditions into account. Could Myanmar take a leaf out of Indian experience of working with federalism? President Thein Sein speaking on the Rakhine Commission Report on 6 May 2013 said: "The Government will also adopt and implement short, medium, and long-term plans to create a harmonious society and achieve economic development in Rakhine state. In doing so, the Government will adopt the recommendations of the Rakhine Investigation Commission as the basis for these plans."[13] However, some scepticism regarding reconciliation under current structures have been expressed. Steinberg says: "The Burman historical efforts to build a nation-state and relegate other ethnic languages and cultures to the intellectual periphery, in a type of balance with their geographical peripheral locations, create continued suspicions among many minority peoples."[14]

Foreign Policy Reforms

In the Ne Win era, Myanmar consciously chose to isolate itself. The SLORC attempts to engage with the rest of the world did not succeed onwards because of the suppression of the democratic upsurge of 1988. The West adopted two-pronged approach of non-engagement and sanctions against Myanmar, provided China the opportunity to fill the void.

Despite China's economic and military inroads in Myanmar, Myanmar itself doesn't want to be overly dependent on any one country. It now has an opportunity to redefine its relations with China in the post-2011, and the post-Myitsone dam period. By developing new economic linkages with ASEAN and countries beyond, Myanmar has been able to develop leverages, which would enable it to exercise greater freedom in its foreign and economic policy.

Neutrality has endured as an important tenet of Myanmar's foreign policy. It was Myanmar's response to domestic, regional and international challenges. Internally, the biggest challenge was ethnic conflict; at the regional level—being placed between two big powers, China and India; and at the global level—interacting in a world divided by two power blocs. The new (2008) Constitution, provides under Article 41: "The Union practices independent, active and non-aligned foreign policy aimed at world peace and friendly relations with nations and upholds the principles of peaceful coexistence among nations."

President Thein Sein delivering his inaugural address before Parliament on 30 March 2011 said "From post-independence period to date, successive governments practised different political and economic policies and concepts. But, regarding the foreign affairs policy, they all exercised non-aligned, independent and active foreign affairs policy and dealt with other countries in line with the Five Principles of Peaceful Coexistence. In addition, they never came under the influence of any powers. They remained neutral in international relations.[15]"

Earlier, Myanmar, through its Declaration 3/88 of 18 September 1988, had signalled its adherence to independent and active foreign policy. Myanmar claims to adhere to equality among people and nations, in accordance with the Five Principles of Peaceful Co-existence that were expounded during Chinese Premier Chou Enlai's visit to Yangon on 28 June 1954.[16]

Myanmar's engagement with the international community has intensified over the last few years.[17] Sanctions that had earlier been imposed against Myanmar are being lifted.

Australia did so in January 2012; the European Union suspended most of them in April 2012; and the "US began to allow American business companies to operate in Myanmar since November 2012."[18]

Myanmar is poised to take over the chairmanship of ASEAN in 2014 and the ASEAN has proposed to establish an integrated ASEAN community (i.e. security, economic and cultural community) by 2015.[19] Hence, the destinies of Myanmar as a nation, and ASEAN as an organization, have got interlinked, and the two may be forced to coordinate their actions.

US Secretary of State, Hillary Clinton, visited Myanmar in early December 2011 and President Obama became the first serving US President to visit Myanmar in November 2012. The President of Myanmar paid a visit to the United States in May 2013. Meanwhile, the US also lifted the ban on Myanmar officials.[20]

Myanmar' foreign policy could not remain untouched by the domestic changes that it was going through. Myanmar's relations with China entered a new phase with the suspension of work on the US$3.6 billion Chinese financed Myitsone hydroelectric dam (at the point where two rivulets converge to form the Ayeyarwady river) in Kachin state on 30 September 2011. This perhaps prompted China to pay greater heed to its relations with Myanmar. China is now attempting to develop ties with not only the political parties, but also ethnic groups. China hosted an NLD delegation for a ten day visit in May 2013 and a multiparty delegation the previous month (April).[21] Myanmar President, at the time of accepting the credentials of the new Chinese Ambassador to Myanmar on 29 March 2013, expressed his government's commitment to support China's "core interests".[22]

Economic Reforms

The effects of colonial economy were deeply felt in Myanmar. Its economy had remained closed during the Ne Win era. Myanmar still does not have a single highway or railroad connection with any of its five neighbours.[23] But the regime has been attempting to attract trade and investment. Myanmar's trade volumes have remained low due to a history of sanctions and boycott by the United States and the European Union. As Myanmar introduces new economic reforms, it will have to factor in the role of ASEAN Free Trade Area agreements with other countries as a possible channel to enhance trade. This includes ASEAN's FTA with China and India. There are additional opportunities in newer forums like Regional Comprehensive Economic Partnership (RCEP) and Trans-Pacific Partnership (TPP). The Greater Mekong Sub Region (GMS) and the BIMSTEC are indicative of the different approaches to economic partnership in the region. Myanmar would draw the key lessons from

Table 1.2: Myanmar: Top 10 Export Partners in 2012 (US Dollars, Millions)

	2003	*2004*	*2005*	*2006*	*2007*	*2008*	*2009*	*2010*	*2011*	*2012*
Thailand	826.96	1230.34	1622.98	2135.72	2104.88	3059.59	2549.02	2590.27	3172.60	3362.58
India	355.24	363.68	450.87	653.09	729.81	829.65	1086.60	1019.09	1143.36	1219.71
PRC Mainland	154.10	188.05	249.49	229.70	336.87	585.93	586.87	873.63	1524.94	1181.20
Japan	126.89	163.47	184.85	225.61	269.20	288.63	309.49	353.40	538.69	612.25
Korea Republic of	26.63	27.36	51.14	87.67	73.35	105.69	71.23	145.36	271.49	319.24
Malaysia	72.62	97.15	121.51	113.53	126.64	162.48	128.68	207.34	212.82	167.56
Vietnam	16.64	17.55	41.64	58.73	68.55	68.73	59.09	93.48	77.09	99.52
Singapore	76.22	64.51	98.53	63.18	55.61	80.03	106.63	74.79	78.01	71.74
Bangladesh	30.21	24.82	29.35	24.45	26.97	75.67	62.27	90.62	141.51	67.85
Korea, DPR	19.33	25.39	29.00	35.85	44.49	50.79	44.43	56.43	63.20	65.89

Source: Direction of Trade Statistics (DOTS)

Data extracted from IMF Data Warehouse on: 6/27/2013 4:02:01 AM the statistics of trade in terms of exports and imports and the balance of trade, and will find out where its national interests really lie.

Myanmar drew a record US$20 billion foreign investment in FY 2010-2011, which is more than what it attracted over the last 20 years. The highest was in oil and gas and electric power, manufacturing, real estate, hotels and tourism, mining, transport and communications. It promulgated the Special Economic Zone Law also. Market forces and the need to supplement Chinese aid compelled Myanmar to begin wooing foreign capital. It's Foreign Investment Law, 1989 sought to streamline procedures, provide guarantees and incentives and allow repatriation of profit. Indonesia had a team of economic advisors called the Berkeley mafia. In Myanmar, which is witnessing a major overhaul of its economic policy (as had occurred in Indonesia), the appointment of Economic Advisors including a former UNESCAP economist (Dr U Myint) may help to frame a more coherent economic policy for the country.

Table 1.3: Basic Economic Indicators: Myanmar

	Myanmar
Population (mn)	64.9
GDP	57.439
GDP per Capita ($)	884.33
Inflation (%)	5.2

Source: IMF.

The World Economic Forum (WEF) has helped Myanmar reintegrate into the international community, and provided another forum to share reform experience with prominent visitors.[24] President Thein Sein, at a meeting with world's leading companies at the WEF on East Asia, said that it was the best time for foreign investors to make investment in Myanmar with the new Foreign Investment Law, which provided protection to investors.[25] Vietnam has seized the opportunity to become the first to invest in Myanmar's hospitality industry with an investment of US$440 million. As many as

62 companies from Ho Chi Minh City participated in the Ho Chi Minh Expo 2013 at Dagon Township in Yangon exhibiting household goods to agricultural machinery.[26] The WEF provides an important opportunity for Myanmar to interact with heads from ASEAN countries, including PM of Laos.

Historically, the horse-shoe of minority-dominated hilly region of Myanmar has suffered from lack of development since colonial times. In order to deal with the challenge of underdevelopment in the conflict-affected areas of the country, there is a need to initiate sustainable development, whose benefits accrue to the local people. In the south, the Dawei project in Tanintharyi Division on the Andaman Sea coast was planned with a deep sea port, an SEZ, and road and infrastructure links with Thailand.[27] With an initial investment of US$13 billion, it was planned to take into account the interest of Karen minority in view besides the Mons and the Burmans, but labour rights concerns and environmental problems could delay the project.[28] While the Thais were entrusted with the development of the Dawei project, the Chinese have undertaken the development of Kyaukphyu deep sea port in the Rakhine state from where the dual-pipeline connecting to Yunnan province also originates. Major Indian ports on the east coast including Chennai and Kolkata would stand to gain with the development of Dawei and Kyaukphyu ports in terms of onward connectivity to the rest of Southeast Asia. The facilities at Sittwe port (also in Rakhine sState) are also being developed as an integral part of the Kaladan project. Once Kaladan project is completed, India's northeast will truly gain from the 'Look East' policy.

Myanmar requires a large aid package, which covers the education and the health sector, especially in the periphery. Education is critical to Myanmar's human resource and skill development, and sustainable and balanced economic growth. The expansion of the civil society and future political leadership depends on it. Aid is a crucial input to good governance. Infrastructure is missing in the periphery—once the road network and accessibility increases, the potential for tourism could be better exploited. There is immense potential for education and exchange programmes to schools, universities and think tanks. Training programmes for government and defence officers could be enhanced.

Myanmar government has also made a number of other economic reforms. It overhauled the exchange-rate system in March 2012 by introducing the managed-float system to stabilise the exchange rate (MK870 per US dollar in August 2012). The Ministry of Commerce replaced the Trade Council for the purpose of granting import/export permits (9 April 2011). The 1988 Foreign Investment law was amended in November 2012 with the enactment of a new Foreign Investment law.

As Myanmar sought to convince the world of the genuineness of its reforms, the EU lifted sanctions on 22 April 2013 while retaining the arms sanctions. A number of European leaders included Myanmar in their itinerary.

Policy Options for India

What options does India have in its Myanmar policy? How much flexibility can India exercise in its options vis-à-vis Myanmar. India's policy is guided by its national interest and Myanmar occupies geostrategic significance. India has an interest in a stable Myanmar. As Myanmar enmeshes itself with the global forces, it will have more reasons to ensure political, economic and social stability within its borders. A key stumbling block to ensuing stability within remains the somewhat uncertain prospects of national reconciliation, especially regarding the Rohingya issue. An unresolved Rohingya problem could come to haunt the neighbours, including India.

Its current approach is pragmatic and India doesn't impose its democratic preferences on others. There are two strands with respect to India's national interest. On the one hand, India desires Myanmar to democratize; on the other, it seeks to ensure (in the face of increasing Chinese influence) that the political transition occurring in Myanmar is as smooth as possible. Experience elsewhere would suggest that externally imposed system has lesser chance of success than an indigenous one. As such, India desires complete democratization in Myanmar in the long term, but knows that the initiative and action for the same has to start amongst the people of that country.

The Way Forward

Myanmar endured military rule for nearly half a century and it progressively came under increasing domestic and international pressure to reform. As Myanmar enmeshes itself with the global forces, it will have more reasons to ensure political, economic and social stability within its borders. A key stumbling block to ensuing stability within remains the somewhat uncertain prospects of national reconciliation, especially regarding the Rohingya issue.

President Thein Sein at a meeting with world's leading companies at the WEF on East Asia said that Myanmar's reform processes are divided into two sections—political and economic and the former could bring about economic development. He said that Myanmar's reforms had four steps: (a) Tatmadaw handing over power to civilian government, (b) ending armed conflict, (c) emergence of good governance and (d) development of private sector.

The nature of the change that was introduced has often been debated. What needs to be understood is that two opposing forces had been at work: the regressive status-quoist forces seeking to retain structures and institutions, and the forces of the future, representing change. The struggle between these forces manifests itself in the political realm, the social realm and the economic realm. In the political realm, it involves a shift from an authoritarian to a democratic state; in the social realm it involves a shift from conflictual relations among the ethnic groups to greater harmony among them; in the economic realm, it involves a transition from a centrally planned economy to a market economy. Should change be measured in quantitative or qualitative terms? Can quantity transform into quality under certain circumstances? If a substantive change has been introduced, it would have many supporters, which may make it difficult to reverse it or overturn it. On the other hand, many small changes could also add up and contribute to the momentum for a lasting change.

Following the end of the Cold War, the old government had been under constant pressure to bring in political and economic reforms. At the same time, the political parties and the ethnic groups were also encouraged to negotiate for reforms in the political system of the country. The military had already formulated its road map to democracy in 2003. According to Min Zin and Brian Joseph: "Burma's rulers appear to have understood even before the Arab Spring came along and reinforced the lesson, that they could no longer simply lash out with force against protest as they had in the past."

The latest Asian Development Bank Report (ADB) predicts that Myanmar could be the next rising star, provided steps for reform proceed in the right direction. The economy was expected to grow (according to ADB) by about 6 per cent in 2012 and 6.3 per cent in 2013. The Economist Intelligence Unit estimates growth at 5.0 per cent in 2012 rising to 7.3 per cent in 2017.

Table 1.4: GDP Growth Estimates

(in percentage)

2012	*2013*	*2014*	*2015*	*2016*	*2017*
5.0	5.5	6.1	6.5	6.9	7.3

Source: The Economist Intelligence Unit, June 2013.

The government attempted to check the high inflation in Myanmar (which, according to ADB, quadrupled between 2001 and 2007 and averaged 25.3%) and scaled it down to a single digit (4.2% in 2011 with an expected rise to 6.2% in 2012).

On the political plane, the two political parties—the USDP and the NLD are confronting the challenge to transform their genetic code, as it were. While the USDP is blessed with a wide-party network, its leadership is deeply introspecting the need to don a new democratic avatar. The NLD, which had been weakened structurally, is now attempting to activate the party neurons and is introspecting the need to adopt a more pragmatic approach (which could, in turn, dilute the idealism of its struggling years). Will the NLD succeed in strengthening its grassroots base and popular appeal? So far the NLD had relied on the iconic appeal of Aung San Suu Kyi, but its organizational structure had suffered in the interim. To revitalize the party, the NLD held its internal elections and convention in March 2013. The NLD now has 1.3 million members.[29] It has 44 seats in the Parliament accounting for 10 per cent of the total. DAASK was elected Chairperson of the NLD. But greater inner party democracy also implies better balance between the "old guard" and the "new blood", something that DAASK acknowledges.[30] The USDP at its party conference in October 2012 acknowledged the need for reform to boost its own chances in 2015 elections. Aung San Suu Kyi's own transition from a symbol of resistance to a parliamentarian requires rather different qualities: indicative of this was her initial hesitation to take a position on important issues, like the Rohingya problem. Independence of the media requires inputs from the media representatives in drafting the Press Law Bill (2013).

Progress on the democratization front depends on change in the constitution. Observers have critiqued the rigid provision for amending the Constitution (requiring 75 per cent majority); Prof. Wojciech Sadurski of the University of Sydney aptly puts it: "If there is an area of consensus emerging… it's that the amendment that is needed is the rule of the amendment."[31] The three priorities in transition to democracy according to DASSK are: upholding rule of law, protection of ethnic minorities and the amendment of the constitution.[32]

Progress on the democratization front is largely predicated on the success of government policy on national reconciliation. The major problems that threaten Myanmar stability is ethnic turmoil. The Rohingya problem in Rakhine state with its fallout in the rest of the country, and the Kachin issue in Kachin state has particularly shaken Myanmar. According to Bertil Lintner, "Rather than being on a path to democracy, Myanmar may find itself instead in the middle of a dangerous and potential volatile superpower rivalry. That means the traditionally powerful military may not be in the mood to give up its dominant role in politics and society any time soon." There could still be some roadblocks on the way; for instance, how will the conservative factions of the military respond to the growing democratization? Could they prove to be a roadblock?[33] How meaningful could the dialogue (talks) between the government and the pro-democracy groups be? Has the government drawn some red lines beyond which it is unwilling to make concessions? This would become evident shortly. The small accretion of strength that the NLD made consequent to the April by-elections, posed no threat to the USDP, which together with the military already controlled about 80 per cent of the seats. When their hold over these 80 per cent seats is threatened that is "probably when the true nature of Myanmar policies on the civilian rule will reveal itself."[34]

Could the international community contribute in a meaningful way to the democratization process?: (a) Japan's commitment to ODA could incentivize the government to introduce political, social and economic reforms. (b) There is scepticism about the process of reform in Myanmar. Even DASSK was not spared for her views on the Latpadaung copper mine and on the Rohingya issue. Abroad, the Southeast Asia scholar Dr. Peter Carey criticized DASSK. "Daw Suu needs to say what needs to be said."[35]

On the economic front, Myanmar has been busy making macro-economic changes to align it with the requirements of dealing with the current economic environment. As Myanmar streamlines its national legislation in line with the international practices, there has been greater willingness on the part of foreign investors to invest in the country. Myanmar introduced the FDI Law in November 2012 and the President sought Parliament's approval to sign the Convention on the Recognition and Enforcement of Foreign Arbitral Awards (or the 1958 New York Convention). This would have to be followed up with new legislation to protect copyright and intellectual property rights.

REFERENCES

1. The pace of change occurring in Myanmar between the two visits in 2012 and 2013 was quite remarkable as was the enthusiasm of the outside world in Myanmar.

2. Available: http://www.altsean.org/Docs/Thein%20Sein%20Speeches/Inaugural%20speech%20to%20National%20Parliament.pdf. Accessed on 25 June 2013.
3. These elections for the national and regional legislatures were contested by 37 political parties, which did not include the NLD and the Shan Nationalities League for Democracy (SNLD). This enabled the military-aligned party, the Union Solidarity and Development Party (USDP) to capture 80 per cent of all legislative seats. Additionally, the Constitution had set aside 25 per cent of the seats for the military.
4. Irrawaddy website, April 3, in BBC Asia Pacific, April 4, 2013.
5. Refer Moe Thuzar, "Myanmar: No Turning Back", in Daljit Singh, Pushpa Thambipillai in *Southeast Asian Affairs 2012*, Institute of Southeast Asian Affairs, Singapore, 2012.
6. These papers are the Union Daily, the Golden Land Fresh Daily, The Voice Daily and The Standard Times.Refer, The Nation, Bangkok, April 1, 2013.
7. Irrawaddy website, March 24, cited in BBC Asia Pacific, March 25, 2013.
8. "Myanmar eases limits on political parties", November 5, 2011. Available: http://www.cbsnews.com/8301-202_162-57319174/myanmar-eases-limits-on-political-parties/. Accessed December 5, 2011.
9. NLD won 43 of the 45 seats in the April by-elections. But, there is yet a huge gap in the number of seats the NLD has and the seats that the largest party, the USDP has in Parliament.
10. *Democratic Voice of Burma* website, March 27, cited in BBC Asia Pacific, March 29, 2013.
11. Pres. Thein Sein Speech to officials from economic and social fields, associations, and organizations, 17 August 2011. Available: http://www.altsean.org/Docs/Thein%20Sein%20Speeches/Speech%20to%20officials%20from%20economic%20and%20social%20fields%20associations%20and%20organizations.pdf. Accessed May 27, 2013.
12. "Burma commission submits report on 2012 Rakhine communal violence", Mizzima News, April 26, in BBC Asia Pacific, April 28, 2013.
13. President Thein Sein's Message on the report of the Rakhine Investigation Commision, 6 May 2013. Available: http://www.altsean.org/Docs/Thein%20Sein%20Speeches/Message%20on%20the%20report%20of%20the%20Rakhine%20Investigation%20Commission%20-%206%20May%202013.pdf. Accessed on 6 June 2013.
14. David I. Steinberg, "The Problem of Democracy in the Republic of the Union of Myanmar", in Daljit Singh, Pushpa Thambipillai in *Southeast Asian Affairs 2012*, Institute of Southeast Asian Affairs, Singapore, 2012.
15. Office of the President of Myanmar website. Available: http://www.president-

office.gov.mm/en/briefing-room/speeches-and-remarks/2011/03/30/id-195. Accessed 27 May 2013.

16. The five principles were; mutual respect for each other's territorial integrity and sovereignty; mutual non-aggression; non-interference in internal affairs; mutual equality and mutual benefit; peaceful co-existence.
17. Myanmar had state level visits from as many as 134 countries or international organizations in 2012 alone.
18. President Thein Sein Message to Parliament, 10 January 2013. Available: http://www.altsean.org/Docs/Thein%20Sein%20Speeches/Message%20to%20National%20Parliament%20-%2010%20January%202013.pdf. Accessed 28 May 2013.
19. Declaration of ASEAN Concord II (Bali Concord II)", Association of Southeast Asian Nations website, October 7, 2003 at www.aseansec.org/15159.htm.
20. "US relaxes visa ban for Burmese officials", in Mizzima news agency, May 3 cited in BBC Asia Pacific, May 4, 2013.
21. The delegation comprised of the All Mon Regional Democracy Party (AMRDP), National Unity Party (NUP), National Democracy Force (NDF), Shan Nationality Democracy Party (SNDP) and Rakhine Nationality Democracy Party (RNDP).
22. Xinhua news agency, March 29, in BBC Asia Pacific March 30, 2013.
23. Lex Rieffel. "Myanmar on the Move: An Overview of Recent Developments," *Journal of Current Southeast Asian Affairs*, vol. 31, no. 4, pp. 31-49.
24. New Light of Myanmar, June 8, 2013.
25. *Ibid.*
26. New Light of Myanmar, June 9, 2013.
27. Ashley South, Prospects for Peace in Myanmar: Opportunities and Threats, PRIO Paper, Oslo 2012.
28. *Ibid.*
29. At the time of NLD's congress in March 2013.
30. Kyodo news service, March 9, cited in BBC Monitoring Asia Pacific, March 10, 2013.
31. Mizzima News Agency, 10 May 2013 cited in BBC Asia Pacific, May 12, 2013.
32. *Ibid.*
33. East Asian Strategic Review 2012, p. 136.
34. *Ibid.,* p. 137
35. Mizzima news Agency, March 18, cited in BBC Monitoring Asia Pacific, March 19, 2013.

2
Reform Process: Achievements and the Way Forward

U. Kyee Myint

The reform process in Myanmar started with the holding of general elections on 7 November 2010. The elections ended the one-party system that prevailed in the country for more than four decades. The elections also restored a Representative Government for the first time in more than two decades. The meeting of the First Pyithu Hluttaw were held on 31 January 2011 and the Speakers were elected. On 4 February 2011, the President and the Vice Presidents were elected. The new government was sworn in at the first meeting of the Pyidaungsu Hluttaw on 30 March 2011. Since then, the winds of change have been sweeping swiftly across the country.

Speed of Change

Changes started with a "remarkable self-critical" inaugural speech of President U Thein Sein. The speed of the changes that followed the elections surpassed the expectations of the people in general as well as the predictions of Myanmar watchers, inside and outside of the country. The President spoke forcefully of the ambitious Reform Agenda, which consists of combating poverty, fighting corruption, ending the country's multiple armed conflicts and working for political reconciliation by highlighting "good governance, clean government" and also highlighted the importance of the role of the media as the fourth pillar. Since then, Myanmar has embarked on a far reaching reform programme to transform the country into a modern, developed and democratic nation that improves the livelihood of its people. Particularly, starting from the month of July 2011, the government has carried out a steady stream of new policies and bold and concrete measures to improve the livelihood of the people and to streamline the administrative processes.

But there are challenges ahead. The main challenges facing the country are to establish political stability, to achieve peace and poverty alleviation. Accordingly, priorities are being given to achieve peace and stability, the rule of law, and socio-economic development for a flourishing democratic system.

Three Stages of Reform Process

The three stages of the reform process are Political Reform, People-oriented Socio-Economic Reform and Administrative Reform of Government Departments and Organizations. The reforms are being undertaken under reform strategies for national development. The government has laid down major development strategies that include strategies to achieve good governance and clean government, to establish inclusive systems and to carry out private sector led development.

Till now, the reforms undertaken by the Government included, amongst others, granting prisoner amnesty and releasing of thousands of prisoners, including prisoners of conscience, starting from 16 May 2011; laying down the Ten Rural Development Tasks at the National level Workshop on Rural Development and Poverty Alleviation held at the Myanmar International Convention Centre on 20 May 2011; and adopting the Eight Poverty Alleviation Tasks at the Rural Development and Poverty Alleviation Central Committee Meeting on 20 June 2011. With regard to rural development and poverty alleviation, the first priority is given to the development of farmers, who account for 70 per cent of the country's total population. Other important reforms carried out by the government also included: Exempted "export tax" on seven export products on 15 August 2011; invited the armed groups to preliminary peace talks on 18 August 2011; reopened dialogue with DASSK with the meeting between President U Thein Sein and Daw Aung San Suu Kyi on 19 August 2011; established the National Human Rights Commission on 5 September 2011; suspended the Myitsone Dam Project on 31 September 2011; granted the second Amnesty and pardoned a total of 6359 prisoners on 11 October 2011; created a National-level Peacemaking Team on 12 December 2011; granted Amnesty to prisoners for the third time on 2 January 2012; announced the rules amending the Political Parties Registration Law on 5 January 2012, to enable the NLD Party to re-enter the political arena; signed a Peace Agreement with the Karen National Union on 12 January 2012; pardoned and released for the fourth time 650 prisoners including a number of prominent dissidents and journalists on 13 January 2012; expanded press freedom conditions on 9 August 2012; called on members of the exile community to return to Myanmar to participate in the national reconciliation efforts, demonstrating that it has been making constant efforts for all inclusiveness in the political process; designed various measures to foster participative public policy debate; legalized labour unions; declared at the 9th Asia-Europe Meeting held in Laos on 6 November 2012 that efforts were being made to reduce Myanmar poverty rate to 16 per cent by 2015 from 26 per cent at present; again granted Amnesty to 518 prisoners on 15-16 November; enacted the Foreign Investment Law in November 2012 to attract foreign investors in the country; formed the Extractive Industry Transparency Initiative Leading Authority on 14 December 2012 to ensure better management for extractive industries of natural resources; approved the Ten Basic Frameworks for Economic and Social Reforms on 27 December 2012; announced on 18 January 2013 an end to the military offensive against the Kachin Independence Army soldiers with effect from 19 January 2013; held peace talks by the Union Level Peace Making Committee with the KIO at Shweli on 4 February 2013; held talks by the Union Peace Working Committee delegation with a delegation of the United Nationalities Federal Council (UNFC) in Chiang Mai on 20 February 2013; formed a Committee in February 2013 to scrutinize the remaining political prisoners serving their terms in the prisons throughout the country, to define the term "prisoner of conscience", to coordinate for a set of framework for scrutinizing and releasing the remaining political prisoners, and to report the findings to the President; drafted necessary economic laws, bylaws, rules and regulations for market competitiveness of exports, reduced export tax and relaxed regulations to ensure flexible situation; and also granted loans to small and medium enterprises as production subsidies to boost the export volume.

Achievements of the Pyithu Hluttaw

In the Pyithu Hluttaw, the opposition parties were able to use their positions creatively to create certain changes. A pattern of lively parliamentary debate has emerged including input of ideas and proposals as well as questioning. The President has formed an Action Committee against Corruption headed by the Vice President for the emergence of good governance and clean government. Following a "good governance and clean government" campaign, between April 2011 and December 2012, some 17,000 civil servants have been punished—with 380 among them being jailed, according to a government report. The Pyithu Hluttaw also formed a Committee on Rule of Law and Tranquillity on 8 August 2012 to overview the rule of law.

The Pyithu Hluttaw has enacted new laws, amended and revoked unpractical laws for the improvement of the rights of labourers and farmers. The members of the Hluttaw also debated the fiscal budget in Parliament for the first time, yielding increased spending in critical areas, such as health, education and infrastructure. Laws to support the development goals of the government have also been passed, including on land reforms, microfinance and foreign investment.

Economic Reforms

The exchange rate regime has been changed from a peg to a managed float. The exchange rate has been stable in recent months, with international reserves increasing to US$ 4 billion. The government has been making efforts for rural development, poverty alleviation and macro economic reform. Out of 50 billion Yen loan to be received from Japan, 10 billion Yen will be used for the rehabilitation of existing power plants, 20 billion for nationwide infrastructure projects, and another 20 billion for the development of the Thilawa special economic zone, about 25 kilometres south of Yangon, which is to be developed by Japanese companies Mitsubishi, Marubeni and Sumitomo. Growth is expected to accelerate to around 6¼ per cent in FY 2012/13, bolstered by foreign investment in natural resources and exports of commodities. Inflation has declined rapidly and should remain moderate at around 6 per cent next year.

Three-Step Peace Making Process

The government laid down three steps in the peace making process. First, ethnic groups are to negotiate a ceasefire with regional-level teams. And then, the talks will move to the Union-level. After that, political talks will be held at the Pyidaungsu Hluttaw.

The government had reached ceasefire agreements with ten major armed ethnic groups out of eleven. The Kachin Independence Organization (KIO) had signed a ceasefire with the previous government in 1994. However, the ceasefire agreement with the KIO had collapsed in June 2011. The government and the Karen National Union (KNU) signed a Ceasefire Agreement on 12 January 2012. On 18 January 2013, the government announced an end to a military offensive against the Kachin Independence Army soldiers, with effect from 19 January 2013. The Union Level Peace Making Committee held peace talks with the KIO on 4 February 2013 at Shweli. The government and the KIO then agreed to continue discussions. The Peace Working Committee delegation also held talks with a delegation of the United Nationalities Federal Council (UNFC) in Chiang Mai on 20 February 2013. The UNFC, formed in early 2011, is an umbrella organization of more than ten ethnic groups. A five-point joint statement was issued at the end of the talks, including an agreement to hold a follow-up meeting within two months.

Relations with the International Community

Myanmar is committed to concentrating on implementing development priorities and plans. The aim is to gain knowledge, experience and resources to facilitate development programmes. The government recognizes its responsibilities towards its citizens and development partners to produce the finest results from international cooperation.

The United States lifted some sanctions on money transfer to Myanmar on 8 May 2012. Canada also suspended most of the sanctions imposed against Myanmar. The Ministry of Labour released a statement in June 2012 that the ILO lifted most sanctions against Myanmar. On 12 July 2012, the US President Mr. Obama announced that economic sanctions against Myanmar were lifted so that US companies could invest in Myanmar as of 11 July 2012. The economic sanctions imposed against the country are now relaxed.

Debt rescheduling agreements with the World Bank, the Asian Development Bank and the Paris Club have been reached. On 17 January 2013, the ADB and the World Bank reissued debt totalling about US$ 960 million through a bridging loan provided by the Japan Bank for International Cooperation (JBIC). On 28 January 2013, the Paris Club, an informal group of creditor governments from major industrialized countries, announced that US$ 5.925 billion debts had been cancelled on 25 January 2013. Remaining arrears will be rescheduled over 15 years, including a seven-year grace period. In addition to the Paris Club's cancellation, Norway and Japan agreed to exceptional debt cancellations, with Norway relieving US$ 534 million and Japan US$3.58 billion. The debt clearance paves the way for new lending. Earlier in January 2013, Japan announced that it would extend loans totalling 50 billion Yen, or about US$ 550 million, to Myanmar.

The IMF is closely assisting the Myanmar government develop and implement the policies to ensure macroeconomic stability and strengthen reforms under their SMP (Staff Monitored Programme). The US Treasury Department, on 22 February 2013, also issued a general license authorizing financial services with four of Myanmar's

Banks: Myanmar Economic Bank, Myanmar Investment and Commercial Bank, Asia Green Development Bank and Ayeyawady Bank.

Cooperation with US Counter-Narcotic Agencies

The Letter of Agreement on Cooperation with Counter-Narcotic Agencies establishing the Opium Yield Survey and Other Purposes between Myanmar and the United States of America was signed on 21 February 2013. By this agreement, Myanmar and the US will carry out a joint opium yield survey in early 2013 and re-establish channels of cooperation on counter-narcotic issues as a means of assisting law enforcement entities of Myanmar in addressing the production and trafficking of opium, and combat transnational crime.

India-Myanmar Relations

An Indian delegation led by the Lok Sabha Speaker Honourable Smt. Meira Kumar visited Myanmar in February 2013. Discussions were held on implementation of Kaladan Project; early completion of India-Myanmar-Thailand highway construction; gearing up repair works of Moreh-Tamu-Kalay-Kalewa-Mandalay route; re-emergence of Lido Road built in WWII that will be of benefit to India, Myanmar and China trade; effective cooperation for ensuring peace and stability in the border region; further cooperation in ICT sector; and boosting cooperation between the two countries and cementing bilateral friendship.

The Way Forward

The reforms are already bearing fruit. Thanks to political and economic reforms, donor countries and international NGOs have increased aids than ever before. There are indications that the international community is committed to support the reform process.

However, Legal Framework and the Rule of Law, infrastructural development, incentives, political stability and competitiveness with neighbours and environmental and social accountability need to be reinforced to be able to invite investments. It is now time for all to extensively engage in the development of socially responsible economy after laying down the economic policies.

The labour issues, farmland disputes, conflicts between environmental degradation and development projects, and communal strife produced a shower of sparks, causing highly sensitive issues. Action is required to put out the shower of sparks as soon as possible before they helped fuel the flames. There are indications that nowadays some sections are encouraging some strata of the people to violate discipline and to commit mob violence. The Rule of Law calls for coordination in accord with the law. Myanmar needs to strive for peace and stability, which are key ingredients for socio-economic development of the country.

The most critical issues or challenges needed to be immediately tackled or overcome by the Myanmar government includes: National Reconciliation: Both Political and Inter-Ethnic Reconciliation; Political Resolution of Armed Conflicts; Inclusive System— Political and Socio-economic; Rule of Law—Security, Economic and Management; Poverty Alleviation; and Economic Development. The factors could help to resolve the issues or overcome the difficulties: Institutional Capacity needs to develop; Inclusive Concept or terminology for National Identity and Foreign Investment.

The developments between now, and 2015 will decide the future course of the country. One question is whether the government will be able to resolve the critical issues the country is encountering without resorting to any fundamental changes. The future developments will give an answer to this question. Whichever way the country moves, there is a very high probability that it would continue to advance towards the goal of building a fully democratized country. For this to happen, the country needs to find ways and means to resolve the fundamental issues. Very recently, President U Thein Sein said: "Democratic reforms could not be delayed or reversed."

3
Myanmar in Transition

Vikash Ranjan

Myanmar is on the threshold of a major political and economic transformation. Politically, it is transiting towards a democratic system and economically, it is moving towards a market economy system. Myanmar has ended one party system, elected a new government, reached agreement for cessation of armed conflicts with eleven major ethnic nationalities, has changed election laws to enable National League for Democracy Party to participate in the electoral processes, debated the fiscal budget for the first time in the Parliament, has renegotiated debts with the World Bank, ADB and Paris Club, has aligned its currency to market forces, and achieved GDP growth rate of 6 per cent. All these reflect reform processes currently underway in the country.

Still, there are many challenges ahead, such as national reconciliation among various ethnic and political groups, socio-economic development challenges and the role of the military in civil administration. Till now, the processes of state formations in Myanmar have failed to integrate ethnic social formations; therefore, the major task before Myanmar is to build national reconciliation with various ethnic groups. The 1948 constitution granted the right to secession to the ethnic minorities, but, it was removed in the 1974 constitution, while the 2008 constitution calls for unity and integrity of the country. The question is whether it would satisfy the ethnic minorities in Myanmar.

Despite abundance of natural resources, Myanmar significantly lags behind its neighbours on most socio-economic indicators. Therefore, the second major challenge that Myanmar faces is to improve socio-economic status of its people. The third challenge that Myanmar faces is 'whether it is possible for the military to hand over power to a civil administration and reconcile to a limited role, as practised by the military in other democratic countries'. Besides, Myanmar faces huge economic and developmental challenges, like poverty, illiteracy and 'fear psychoses' against the ruling regime, with significant illegal economy based on smuggling of drugs, gemstones and the need to establish civil societies.

Myanmar's assumption of ASEAN chair in 2014 is significant. The assumption of ASEAN chair by Myanmar would break its long isolation from the international community. As final preparations for the realization of an ASEAN Economic Community in 2015 would be made during Myanmar's chairmanship, this event will accelerate Myanmar's economic development. Myanmar is already a member of the World Trade Organization.

Key Protagonists

The military (*Tatmadaw*), the pro-democracy supporters led by Aung San Suu Kyi, different ethnic parties/groups, and the Buddhist clergy are the key protagonists. Ethnically, Myanmar has 60-65 per cent Burmans and the rest comprise of several ethnic groups like Shan, Karen/Kayin, Mon, Rakhine, Chin, Kachin, Karenni/Kayah, Wa, Rohingya, Kokang, Lahu, Danu, etc. There are more than 100 languages and dialects in Myanmar. Buddhism is the major religion in Myanmar with 85 per cent of followers, therefore Buddhist clergies, who have played a crucial role in the nationalist movement, and pro-democracy movements, are a major force to reckon with.[1] While the majority Burmans are Thervada Buddhists, the majority of ethnic Kachin and Chin and a significant minority of Karen are Christians.

Political Reforms

Myanmar has witnessed a number of political developments in recent years. Myanmar drafted a new Constitution (2008), held a referendum for approving it, organized elections (union and state legislatures) and put in place a new Parliament and Government. Under the new Constitution, some positive changes have begun to unfold like the release of pro-democracy leader, Ms. Aung San Suu Kyi and a number of political prisoners, establishment of the Human Rights Commission; freedom of speech including the Internet; suspension of work on the Myitsone hydroelectric power project; and the permission to form unions and go on strike; reflects the government's pro-people overtures.

However, the most crucial test for Myanmar will come in 2015 elections. How the military will loosen its hold on power after the elections needs to be seen. The present constitution preserves 25 per cent of seats for the military in the 664-member Parliament. In addition, the President wields enormous powers.

Earlier, the pro-democracy group led by the National League for Democracy (NLD) won the 1990 general elections with 59 per cent of the national votes and 81 per cent (392 out of 485) of the seats of Parliament. However, the military government did not recognise the elections and imprisoned many of its leaders including Aung San Suu Kyi. A number of elected representatives escaped arrest and formed the National Coalition Government of the Union of Burma, the government in exile, headquartered in Manerplaw along the Thai-Burmese border.

Even after the by-elections in which NLD participated and won 43 out of 45 seats, dispute arose over oath of office, sparking a political crisis, as the party wanted wording in the oath changed from 'safeguard' to 'respect' the Constitution, which they have vowed to amend because it enshrines military power. However, as the army representatives wield enormous powers, and changes to the Constitution require a 75 per cent majority, it is difficult to change any aspect of the Constitution without military's approval.

Nevertheless, dissidents of the 1988 generation, who were the bitterest opposition to the military rule, are feeling that there are changes underway in the country, as they can operate independently, without being followed around by military spies. Journalists, who had never thought that they could return home after years in exile, have set up offices in Yangon and even engaged with the government. Representatives of various democratic parties, which participated in the 2010 elections, claim that they have been able to raise controversial issues in the legislature. Besides, many political prisoners have been freed, reflecting that the Myanmar government is serious in its reform process, and the country is witnessing a new dawn.

Myanmar's media have been one of the most assertive sectors of Myanmar society since the democratic reforms began in the country. With the reform process underway in Myanmar, the censorship of the media has been loosened gradually. Private publications in Myanmar have thrived since President Thein Sein began taking steps to open up the country's economy and move towards democracy. Gradually, articles dealing with entertainment, health, children, sports, economics, crime, legal affairs, education, religion and politics have been freed from censorship in the course of time. The government in a statement on 20 August 2012 said that "All publications in Myanmar are exempt from the scrutiny of Press Scrutiny and Registration Department",[2] was a very significant step.

The Myanmar Journalists Association, which has 800 members, held its first congress on 11 August 2012 and told government officials that they were not welcome. A series of changes, including a press law being drafted by the government, would allow Myanmar a level of press freedom unimaginable during the days of the military rule. However, Myanmar media still exercises some self-censorship on issues like, military affairs, ethnic conflicts, corruption, etc. In a society that has been closed for decades, citizens have learnt the value of discretion.

However, sceptics have raised questions like: What is the motive for the Military to bring the political change and whether it is sustainable? In 2003, the military regime announced a seven-step "road map to disciplined democracy", and changes have been brought in tune with this. Several analysts believe that the military has broadly followed the road map as its "safest exit strategy." Under this framework, it continues to retain the levers of power both inside and outside the Parliament, and can determine the pace of change. The roadmap has allowed the regime to broaden its social base and insulate it from any rude shock, which they otherwise might have had to face. It is opined that as the capacity building of the population is required to replace military administration, the transition process to civil administration will be slow till there are enough expertise in the country to take the uphill governance task.

But others emphasize on the role of external actors like ASEAN for the change. Myanmar has begun to lag behind even Laos, Vietnam and Cambodia in its socio-economic indicators. Cyclone Nargis and increasing fear of becoming China's satellite state may also have contributed in changing the attitude of Myanmar ruling regime that they need to diversify foreign policy options, and expand ties with the western countries. However, this was only possible with democratic reforms, and for the reforms to have any credibility, it needed Aung San Suu Kyi's support so that the world would take it seriously. In that context, Ms Aung San Suu Kyi's landmark meeting with the President in August 2011 can be seen after which she decided to engage with the political process.

Ethnic Issues

Myanmar was ruled by the military government for most of the time since getting independence in 1948. The strong ethnic identities of the people nurtured by political and economic interests limited Myanmar's evolution as a cohesive and integrated society, providing excuses for military interventions. Therefore, the biggest challenge that Myanmar faces is the task of national reconciliation among ethnic groups. The processes of state formations in Myanmar have failed to fully integrate the ethnic social formations, which is a herculean task, which need to be addressed to fructify the reform process.

Owing to the internal conflicts and human rights abuses, many people became displaced in their own country, or, took refuge in the neighbouring countries, like Thailand, China, Bangladesh and India. Upholding the rights of all ethnic groups is crucial for national reconciliation and political stability. For this, they need to have an independent and effective judiciary.

For example, the Shan State Army South agreed to a ceasefire with the government in December 2011 in response to peace overtures from the President Thein Sein.[3] It had been one of the biggest rebel groups fighting Myanmar's army, mostly from guerrilla outposts bordering Thailand, for greater autonomy for decades. The mainly Buddhist Shan are the country's second-biggest ethnic group, accounting for about nine per cent of the population, and the Shan state covers a vast area of north eastern Myanmar. The Chin Human Rights Organization alleged that Chins are forced to convert to Buddhism, despite claims that religious freedom is protected.[4] Poverty among the Chins, who depend on farming, leaves the group vulnerable.[5]

Insurgency, guerrilla warfare, rugged nature of the terrains, cross border support for insurgents due to ethnic affinities in neighbouring countries are some of the major asymmetric warfare factors in Myanmar. Due to porosity of the borders, the insurgent groups take shelter in the neighbouring areas making any operations against them by the Myanmarese government difficult, and providing it a trans-national character, as evidenced in Kachin insurgents' affinity with China, and that of Rohingyas with Bangladesh and other Islamic countries.

However, in Myanmar, no country is supposed to be directly involved in fanning the conflict. Still different ethnic and support groups in neighbouring countries like China, Bangladesh, India, Thailand, and some Buddhist, Islamic, and Christian religious organizations have sympathy for people along ethnic and religious lines.

Case Study of Rohingya

The violence in Rakhine state erupted after a Buddhist girl was raped by three Rohingyas, and subsequent retaliation by Buddhists, resulting in a number of Rohingyas crossing into Bangladesh. It led Indonesia to delay the state enterprises to seek business opportunities in Myanmar.[6] In Bangaldesh, the Rohingya refugee influx started in 1978 after a military operation known as 'Nagamin Dragon' to suppress an uprising.[7]

A photo of Tibetan monks standing in front of a pile of dead bodies appeared in many countries, especially Pakistan. It was later taken off the website; but, was still in circulation, and appeared in Zee News, India. The Dalai Lama's government in exile denounced the use of misleading photo to whip up anti-Buddhist sentiment in the Muslim world. The photo actually was of a relief work in Kyegudo

(Yushul), eastern Tibet, after a devastating earthquake hit the region on 14 April 2010, when the Tibetan monks provided service in the rescue and relief operations.[8]

Bangladesh in 2012 refused to allow in Rohingya Muslims fleeing ethnic clashes in coastal Rakhine state, sending their boats back. Bangladeshi officials said that the country could not host more Rohingya. Sending the refugees back into danger is illegal under international law. But, Bangladesh is not the only nation that has been charged with pushing back people fleeing Myanmar. Later in the year, China was alleged to have expelled 5,000 ethnic Kachin people, who fled fighting between rebels and Myanmar troops, according to the United Nations refugee agency, calling on China to protect and shelter the displaced people.[9]

The potential area for organized crimes with links to international terrorist organisation can come in Arakan State having significant Rohingya population. The UN describes the Rohingya as one of the world's most persecuted minorities. The immediate challenge for the international community is to ensure that the conflict affected displaced Rohingya people are safe and have access to basic needs like, food, shelter and medical care. Otherwise, terrorist organisations like al-Qaeda and other organisations will find them ready fodder to serve their purpose. The Pakistani Taliban group Tehreek-e-Taliban recently made a threat against Myanmar announcing that they will take revenge of their blood for the treatment meted out to the Rohingya. This is the first time that Tehreek-e Taliban has publicly threatened Myanmar.

Myanmar rejected ASEAN chair's call for an urgent meeting on Rohingya while granting access to the Organization of Islamic Cooperation and UN agencies. Myanmar has sent mixed signals to ASEAN; for example, it has maintained a distance with ASEAN on the South China Sea dispute and the Rohingya issue. On August 10, 2012, Myanmar's Foreign Minister, Wunna Maung Lwin, received a letter from the Cambodian Foreign Minister, Hor Namhong calling for a special meeting on the Rohingya without prior consultation. Myanmar claimed that the letter was "a total surprise" and quickly turned down the offer. Indonesia and Thailand, which initially supported the idea, later backed out. A week later, ASEAN agreed to issue a joint statement on the situation in the Arakan state without calling a special meeting.[10]

The Rohingya are facing a humanitarian disaster, increasingly alienated from the administrations of Burma and Bangladesh; if the international community is unwilling to take immediate action to assist them, it would hardly be surprising if they feel forced to turn elsewhere for help.

Economy

Myanmar's economy has remained closed for about two decades. Still, the market forces and the need to supplement Chinese aid compelled the country to woo foreign capital in the form of trade and investment. In FY 2010-2011, Myanmar drew a record US$ 20 billion foreign investment mostly from China and Thailand, which was more than what it attracted over the last 20 years. The highest was in oil and gas and electric power, manufacturing, real estate, hotels and tourism, mining, transport and communications. It promulgated the Special Economic Zone Law also. Nevertheless, Myanmar's Foreign Investment Law 1989 needs to streamline procedures, provide guarantees and allow repatriation of profits.

There is favourable investment climate in Myanmar with 6.25 per cent GDP growth rate in 2011-12, which is expected to go up to 7 per cent or more in the next five years. Myanmar has allowed 100 per cent Foreign Investment in most of the sectors with some exception. There is no minimum cut off for the investments, and they have allowed land lease for 50 years with provision of extension twice for 10 years each, with 5 year tax exemptions. All these show that Myanmar is rich in agricultural and natural resources, where wage labour is very competitive and has huge potential for growth.

As by 2015, the ASEAN free trade integration of member states, which fully liberalizes trade throughout the region is about to take place, investors interested in Myanmar need to fully understand ASEAN integration process, as it will benefit companies setting up a holding company in other member countries of ASEAN, such as Vietnam, Indonesia, Thailand, till Myanmar is in the catching up process. Since theMyanmar government has allowed Banks from the ASEAN region to set up operational branches by 2014, and banks from other countries will be able to establish joint ventures within the same time-frame, the hindrances in direct trading with Myanmar would be removed. Still, the regulatory and procedural legislation and structure is yet to be worked out. As Singapore is already a world class financial and services hub, the investments in Myanmar can be routed through it. Investors can also take advantage of lower income tax and double tax agreement benefits for trade with China and India, the two fastest emerging Asian economies. Moreover, the ASEAN+3 Asian Bond Markets Initiative holds much potential for Myanmar.

Till the beginning of the reform process, the authoritarian nature of the governance limited its capacity for fuller utilization of natural and human resources, by creating overtly centralized and localized economies, in tune with the elite's interests. They devolved much administrative and economic decision making to regional commanders, who are said to have developed strong regional economic interests and have built powerful local political bases. As such, Myanmar needs to steadily establish civilian control over the military, take over its businesses and begin professionalising its ranks.

Moreover, Myanmar faces huge development challenges. Agriculture remains mainstay in Myanmar's economy and society, accounting for around 58 per cent of the country's GDP, 48 per cent of its exports and provides employment to two-thirds of the population. Despite the abundance of natural resources, Myanmar is low income country, as GDP per capita of Myanmar stood at some US$ 1,400 in 2012.[11] However, due to its isolation from the International Financial Institutions and regional development banks, reliable and quality data is not available for an objective assessment of socio-economic development in Myanmar. Myanmar is significantly lagging behind its neighbours on most socio-economic indicators on poverty, health and education, with a Human Development Index ranking of 149 out of 187 countries in 2012.[12] On Transparency International Index 2012, Myanmar ranks 172 out of 176 countries on the Corruption index.[13] There is a significant illegal economy that is based on smuggling of drugs, gemstones, timber, etc. Ignorance of economic correlations and international isolation has undermined the prospects for robust economic development in the country. For optimizing the impact of development assistance, Myanmar needs to develop an effective system of governance and infrastructure.

Drugs

Myanmar is the world's second-largest opium poppy grower after Afghanistan. Myanmar's multiple ethnic rebel organisations generally use profits from narcotics to fund their operations. The total opium-poppy cultivation area in Myanmar in 2012 was estimated at 51,000 hectare, a 17 per cent increase from the 43,600 hectare cultivation area in 2011. In 2012, potential opium production increased by 13 per cent to 690 metric tonnes. During the year, an estimated 300,000 households were involved in opium poppy cultivation in Myanmar.

Myanmar was branded as a major source of methamphetamine pills and opiates in Southeast Asia, by a UN Office on Drugs and Crime (UNODC) report in 2011, where it labelled the Shan state as a production hub for drugs in Myanmar.[14] Recently, Myanmar's government and Shan ethnic rebels signed a deal to wipe out opium and amphetamine production in the state, a notorious drugs hub bordering Thailand. Rebel negotiators had called for a cross-border blitz on drug production, urged funds to be made available to poppy farmers, who abandon the crop and for traffickers to be punished. The rebels have also pledged to cooperate with neighbouring China, Laos and Thailand to control the cross-border movement of chemicals used to make the pills, often in small factories hidden in the jungle. According to the Shan Drug Watch 2012, if political settlement of long-standing ethnic dissatisfaction is not reached, the armed conflict that fuels Burma's drug epidemic will never end. According to some political analysts, poppy growing and opium production in the Shan state have increased over the past two years due to political volatility in Burma and growing economic despondency caused by cronyism, corruption and unprofessional conduct of the government.

However, other ethnic groups are also involved in producing the drugs. A senior Thai politician, Chalerm Yubamrung, the Deputy Prime Minister in charge of a nationwide blitz on drugs accused neighbouring Myanmar of failing to tackle drug production after 3.3 million amphetamine tablets were seized in Bangkok. The haul, with a street value of US$ 350,000 and believed to be one of the biggest on record in Thailand, is believed to be produced by the Wa ethnic group in Myanmar. The Wa live in an autonomous region in northern Shan state bordering China and Laos, and are believed to have a thousand strong army that is sustained by the drug money. He is also reported to have said that he will ask China to exert its influence on Myanmar, and blamed the Taiwanese and Indian manufacturers for an influx of base chemicals used to make synthetic drugs and hit out at human rights groups, who oppose his idea of swift execution for convicted drug traffickers. Thailand's Office of Narcotics Control Board (ONCB) says that nearly 360,000 people were arrested on drugs charges over the last year, while 72.5 million amphetamine pills have been seized in that period.[15]

Unless the ethnic issues are sorted out, drugs trade will take place, because drug is a kind of weapon for local leaders for grabbing power.

International Community

Myanmar's stand on the Myitsone project suggests that the country is ready to break ranks with its ally and powerful neighbour China, and engage with the international community. Myanmar's Minister for Science and Technology announcement on 23 September 2011,[16] to abandon plans to build nuclear technology as it may cause concern to the international community echoes the country's desire to jettison its political and economic isolation, and start a new chapter in the country's history.

ASEAN, other major powers like US, EU, India, Japan, have started enhancing their stakes in the country. US has announced to ease economic sanctions and investment ban from the country and has suspended sanctions on export of American financial services and investment across all sectors of the Myanmar economy—including in the oil, gas and mining sectors. As other Western nations and the European Union had already taken similar moves, putting pressure on US to do likewise so that US companies would not lose out to foreign competitors in Myanmar's market. The ban on financial transactions had been a particular hurdle for doing business in Myanmar, since the dollar is the world's main trading currency, and transactions through other currencies raised costs to uncompetitive levels. If US companies invest in Myanmar, it will get technology, new markets and management skills, which will lead to further growth of the country. US companies will also be able to help Myanmar to sell its products in larger global export market. However, despite the easing of restrictions, the US has still barred companies from doing business with firms associated with the country's powerful military.

The EU has also lifted sanctions from the country and is encouraging its member States to develop economic engagements with Myanmar. The European Union has given various aid packages for improvement of health, education and training in Myanmar. Japan has pledged to provide 600 billion yen (US$ 7.5 bn) of official development assistance in the three years starting fiscal 2013 to the five countries of the Mekong River region Myanmar, Thailand, Cambodia, Laos and Vietnam. Japan's decision to forgive, in stages, 300 billion yen of its past yen loans to Myanmar and supply fresh lending to the country for the first time in 25 years. India has offered around US$ 500 million in credit to Myanmar to help develop its infrastructure, such as railways, roads and waterways, and it is also helping Myanmar in building a port in the coastal Myanmar city of Sittwe. India hopes that Sittwe port will act as a trade gateway between India's north-eastern states and ASEAN countries. As China has made huge investments in Myanmar, and Myanmar is strategically important from China's perspective also, Myanmar's widening engagement with US, the European Union and other powers has concerned China. It can be inferred from the fact that China blamed the US for the suspension of Myitsone dam project worth US$ 3.6 billion. China perceives US engagement with Myanmar as a direct challenge to it in its own backyard.

India-Myanmar Relations

India's policy in Myanmar is guided by national interest and geostrategic significance. The two neighbouring countries have shared historical, ethnic, cultural and religious ties. The collective memory and history of rich connections and exchanges through trade, culture, religious influences and ideas has provided the basis for bridging of relationships.

India's relations with Myanmar are guided by New Delhi's 'Look East' policy, which has served as an important tool of its foreign policy. Myanmar is India's immediate neighbour and shares a long border of 1,643 km with India's northeast region and maritime borders in the Bay of Bengal region. For India, the strategic partnership with Myanmar is undoubtedly one of the most important external relationships. Sardar K.M. Panikar in his book, "The Future of India and Southeast Asia," published in 1945, wrote that "The defence of Burma is, in fact, the defence of India and it is India's primary concern no less than Burma's to see that its frontiers remain inviolate. In fact, no responsibility can be considered too heavy for India when it comes to the question of defending Burma." Myanmar is scheduled to chair ASEAN in 2014 and this period will further reinforce New Delhi's engagement with Nay Pyi Taw.

Myanmar has the potential to become a convenient transit route for India's growing trade relations with Southeast Asia. Besides ASEAN, India and Myanmar are also cooperating at sub-regional levels, like the Mekong Ganga cooperation (MGC), BCIM and BIMSTEC. Myanmar is also an observer in SAARC.

India has a stake in seeking cooperation of Myanmar for developing its north-east region. The north-east people want economic development and security. They have relatives across borders in Myanmar. As there is no dearth of raw materials in the region, consumer, engineering and food-processing industries may be set up in the region benefitting people on both sides of the border. For India, large quantities of unexploited oil and gas reserves of Myanmar can be useful in meeting its energy security, for developing its north-east region, for maintaining its internal security, etc.

In the economic sector, India-Myanmar bilateral trade has

expanded significantly from US$ 12.4 million in 1980-81 to reach US$ 1870.2 million in 2011-12, which has more than trebled from 2005 to 2006 figures of US$ 569.17 million. The balance of trade has always been in favour of Myanmar. India is the fourth largest trading partner of Myanmar after Thailand, Singapore and China. India's main export to Myanmar consists of primary and semi-finished steel and pharmaceuticals; while its main import consists of agricultural items, like beans, pulses and forest-based products.

An important component of India-Myanmar trade consists of border trade. Though the official border trade between the two countries seems very marginal, the unofficial border trade based on head load basis has been reported to be very high, almost in comparison with the regular trade. Two border trade points, Moreh-Tamu (1995) and Zowkhathar-Rhi (2004) have become operational so far with an agreement to open a third trade point, Avakhung-Leshi. Cotton yarn, auto parts, pharmaceuticals and soybean meal from India; and pulses, dried ginger, betel nuts, turmeric from Myanmar have been the main items of exchange through the border trade points.

The Government of India is actively involved in over a dozen projects in Myanmar, both in infrastructural and non-infrastructural areas. These include upgradation and resurfacing of the 160 km long Tamu-Kalewa-Kalemyo road; construction and upgradation of the Rhi-Tiddim road in Myanmar; the Kaladan Multimodal Transport Project; etc. India can offer to establish "development corridors" along these routes with backward and forward linkages, which would be beneficial for bringing growth in both the countries.

ONGC Videsh Ltd. (OVL), GAIL and ESSAR and others, are participants in off-shore and on-shore blocks, and construction of natural gas pipelines in the Bay of Bengal region. In generating electricity from renewable energy sources, both the countries agreed to encourage their domestic public and private sector companies to set up joint projects. In September 2008, Ministry of Electric Power-1 (MoEP-1) and NHPC signed an agreement for the development of the Tamanthi and Shwezaye Hydro-Electric Power project in Chindwin River valley and NHPC submitted the updated DPR on Tamanthi and is working on the DPR on the Shwezaye project. Both countries have also agreed to enhance cooperation in renewable energy sources including solar and wind.

M/s RITES is involved in the development of the rail transportation system and in supply of railway coaches, locos and parts. A heavy turbo-truck assembly plant set up in Myanmar by TATA Motors with GOI financial assistance was inaugurated on December 31, 2010. An India-Myanmar Industrial Training Centre has been set up by HMT(I) in Myanmar with the assistance of GOI in Pakokku, a second centre is being set up in Myingyan, while the Myanmar-India Centre for English Language (MICELT), a Myanmar-India Entrepreneurship Development Centre (MIEDC) and an India-Myanmar Centre for Enhancement of IT Skills (IMCEITS) are all operational. An ADSL project for high speed data link in 32 Myanmar cities has been completed by TCIL. Other projects include revamp of the Ananda Temple in Bagan, upgradation of the Yangon Children's Hospital and Sittwe General Hospital, erection of disaster proof rice silos, etc[17]. India has also assisted in the reconstruction of one high school and six primary schools in Tarlay township, the area worst affected by the severe earthquake that struck the north-eastern Myanmar in March 2011.

India and Myanmar need to establish a Trade and Investment Forum at the business level, open up new border trading points for the economic upliftment of the local people, expand the basket of goods under border trade, open up more Indian banks branches in the country to facilitate better trade and payment arrangements between the two countries. India needs to urge business associations in respective countries to enhance ties with their likely counterparts in each other's country and participate in trade fairs.

However, there is concern about delay in implementation of projects between the two countries. Both countries need to analyse this from other country's perspective and work on strengths while mitigating the shortcomings. The proposed economic corridors need to be turned into industrial, infrastructural development corridors with forward and backward linkages for the benefit of local community.

Still, there is huge scope for both countries to cooperate in food, water security and other areas. For enhanced economic relations, both countries need to develop Border Area development projects and set up Border trade committee, and open more and more border haats. They should not allow third country goods to come through border haats. There is a need to increase Rail, Road, Air and Shipping connectivity between the two countries. There is scope for cooperation for Small and Medium enterprises between the two countries. The banking sector cooperation between the two countries needs to be enhanced. A feasibility study for Kyaukphyu Special Economic Zone, opportunities for participation of Indian companies in Thilawa, Dawei and other SEZs needs to be explored. There is opportunity for owning up existing companies in various sectors like rice, sugar and pulp, engineering, plywood, paper, pulp, auto, etc., which can be explored. However, in these types of transactions, the question arises as to how to evaluate the existing companies; because if it is very high, it is a disincentive for investor, if it is very low, local politics cry foul over selling of national resources.

Conclusion

Myanmar has taken a number of positive steps for the growth and development of the country, and has provided opportunities to both endogenous and exogenous forces to engage and reinforce positive trends in the country. This will break the shackles of wide range poverty and conflicts in the country. The international community, particularly the political and business class need to grab the opportunities presented in the virgin land and bring it back as a responsible member in the comity of nations. This will herald peace, stability and growth both for Myanmar and the wider region.

REFERENCES

1. Schearf, D., Authorities Nurture Burma's Buddhist Chauvinism Analysts Say, http://www.voanews.com/content/burma_buddhist_chauvinism_nurtured_by_authorities/1503665.html. Accessed 8 September 2012.
2. Thomas Fuller, Myanmar to curb censorship of the Media, The New York Times, http://www.nytimes.com/2012/08/21/world/asia/myanmar-abolishes-censorship-of-private-publications.html?_r=0. Accessed 22 August 2012.

3. Linn, Z., Can President make completely peaceful Burma? http://asiancorrespondent.com/88947/can-president-make-completely-peaceful-burma/. Accessed 10 September 2012.
4. Myanmar Christians forced to convert to Buddhism: Rights group, The Express Tribune. http://tribune.com.pk/story/431776/myanmar-christians-forced-to-convert-to-buddhism-rights-group/. Accessed 6 September 2012.
5. In Brief: Chins denied religious freedom in Myanmar, IRIN Asia. http://www.irinnews.org/Report/96244/In-Brief-Chins-denied-religious-freedom-in-Myanmar. Accessed 6 September 2012.
6. Siahaan, T. Indonesia Spurns Investment in Burma over Rohingya Crisis, Jakarta Globe. http://www.irrawaddy.org/archives/13471. Accessed 8 September 2012.
7. Bashar, I., Rohingyas: A Quest for a Sustainable Solution. http://www.nationmultimedia.com/opinion/Rohingyas-A-Quest-for-a-Sustainable-Solution-30184813.html. Accessed 26 June 2012.
8. OIC team to probe violence against Rohingya Muslims, (2012), Saudi Gazette.com.sa. http://www.saudigazette.com.sa/index.cfm?method=home.regcon&contentid=20120906135263. Accessed 7 September 2012.
9. China chastised for sending Kachin people back to Myanmar, Los Angeles Times. http://latimesblogs.latimes.com/world_now/2012/09/china-chastised-for-sending-kachin-people-back-to-myanmar.html, Accessed 8 September 2012.
10. Chongkittavorn, K., Naypyidaw Sending Mixed Signals to Asean, The Nation, 3rd September. http://www.irrawaddy.org/archives/13131. Accessed 17 August 2013.
11. CIA The World Fact Book. https://www.cia.gov/library/publications/the-world-factbook/geos/bm.html.
12. UNDP, International Human Development Indicators. http://hdrstats.undp.org/en/countries/profiles/MMR.html. Accessed on 25 March 2013.
13. Transparency International, Corruption Perception Index. http://www.transparency.org/country#MMR. Accessed 16 September 2013.
14. Shan vow to wipe out drugs (2012), Bangkok Post, May 19. http://www.bangkokpost.com/breakingnews/294163/shan-vow-to-wipe-out-drugs.
15. Thai official calls on Burma to address amphetamine production, Democratic Voice of Burma. http://www.dvb.no/news/thai-official-calls-on-burma-to-address-amphetamine-production/23649. Accessed 16 September 2012.
16. Lynn, Soe Than, Minister denies nuke rumours, The Myanmar Times. http://www.mmtimes.com/2011/news/595/news59518.html. Accessed 30 March 2012.
17. India-Myanmar Relations, Ministry of External Affairs, Accessed over a period of time from July- August 2013.

4
Ethnic Minorities, Nation Building and the Road to Democracy

Pankaj Jha

Myanmar has been incrementally subscribing to the concept of democracy and calibrated political reforms. If the parliamentary elections and people's participation are the parameters, then the results can be construed as positive. However, the bigger question is whether a country devoid of any democratic institutions and structures for a long time can sustain an embryonic edifice. More importantly, the challenge is the nation building and assimilation of the ethnic minorities in the mainstream, so as to streamline efforts with regard to development, growth and political participation. The scepticism still lingers about the sincerity of military junta to allow civilian government formation in future and how that transition would take place in the long run. However, the military junta is not the only accused for adopting lacklustre approach; in fact, the western media has also used religion and ethnicity for their vested interests, creating further fissures within the fragmented society. This chapter addresses the challenges for the ethnic minorities as well as government to reach a meeting ground and how it will contribute to the nation building process.

In the historical context, pre-modern states have existed in the central riverine plains of Myanmar since at least the eighth century AD. Burman kings established 'empires' centred at Bagan (11th-13th centuries), Toungoo (14th-16th centuries) and Ava (18th-19th centuries), ruling over a diverse array of ethno-linguistic groups. The two dominant cultures were Bamar and Mon, and at the time of British incursion in the 19th century, the Bamar Kingdom, centred at Amarapura and later Mandalay, had conquered the other states as well as Arakan (Rakhine) on the western coast. True to the *Mandala* concept, the smaller principalities in the Shan region owed allegiance to the dominant Bamar court, as did some of the lesser ethno-political entities in the mountainous arc at the rim of the riverine plains.[1] This laid to the foundation of the modern Myanmar. However, the Britishers, during their governance, promoted sub-nationalism within Burma to suit their interests, which in a way created problems in nation building in Burma.

Nation Building in Myanmar

Anthony Smith defines the nation as "a named human population, which shares myths and memories, a mass public culture, a designated homeland, economic unity, and equal rights and duties for all members".[2] The term of nation-building originates from the English language, which was popularized by the Western society as they were the ones, who conceptualized the notion. Before a nation could be founded, there are five elements that must be fulfilled. One of the aspects is that the country must have gained independence. Second, the society should have solidarity, which could motivate its people into governing the country. Third, there should be an organized political system, which provides space for a government to carry out their responsibilities. The fourth element is that, the country must have autonomy, where the government has the authority to endorse, grant consent, demand loyalty and support to make the country's administration more systematic. Fifth, the government-of-the-day must have the people's mandate. The people must be loyal and support the government, at least to work towards achieving political unity or become a member of the country, where the pact will continue even when the government faces crisis. The process of nation-building is an effort to develop the spirit of patriotism and solidarity to create a country whose people share a common identity.[3] As an alternate view, nation building, according to Jochen Hippler, consists of three major elements:

1. An integrative ideology that might be nationalist, but could also be religious, racist, developmentalist or shaped along other lines, as long as it provides for integrating the sub-groups of the inhabitants of a country into one society.
2. An integrated society, with its several elements, communicating more often with each other than with outsiders. This implies a 'nationwide' integration of geographic regions, economic sectors and politics. It also presupposes a functioning infrastructure and intellectual discourse of 'national' scale.
3. An existing state apparatus, which actually fulfils its functions on all of the national territory.[4]

The major aim of nation building is to foster national unity by developing a new nation and an integrated race. In Malaysia, the idea of establishing a nation was initiated before the Malayan Union was introduced during the struggles for seeking independence from British colonization. One of the initiatives was the concept of '*Negara-Cita Melayu*' with the slogan *Melayu-Raya* that involved the collaboration of nationalists in Malaya and Indonesia. The tie was made stronger as they share many common cultural elements, such as religion, language, traditions, political system and economic background.[5] Myanmar, which was also a British colony, failed in undertaking these measures as it failed in generating debate about the nation and the benefits of nation building. This can be attributed to the death of its revered leader Aung San and the intermittent efforts from the subsequent military governments to initiate dialogue with the ethnic minorities. The ethnic differences were also the fallout of the historical legacy and the divisive British policy towards these minorities.

Established as a functioning democracy after independence from Britain in 1948, Burma (as it was known then) saw a barely constitutional caretaker government take office for 18 months in the late 1950s and witnessed a full-blown military coup in 1962. For nearly half a century since then, it has not succeeded in restoring democracy, although nationwide protests in 1988, a general election in 1990 and a monk-led 'saffron uprising' in 2007[6] indicated that there was ample support for doing so. Indeed, democracy talk now dominates political debate to such an extent that the military junta acceded to the demand for a general election in 2010. Under successive authoritarian regimes, nationalism has remained a central feature of the political landscape. For six decades of this sovereign state, the political agenda has thus been dominated by problems of democratization and nationalist conflict.[7] However, these ethnic conflicts were intrinsic to the national structure of Myanmar given the diverse sub-nationalism, which was supported by the colonial masters.

Ethnic Fissures and Sub-nationalism

Comprizing more than 135 different ethnic groups, each with its own history, culture and language, Myanmar has been facing challenges in the form of national assimilation, economic growth and sustainable development. This can be attributed to the colonial legacy and the British policy of 'divide and rule' in the Indian sub-continent.[8]

The majority Burman (Bamar) ethnic group accounts for about two-thirds of the population and controls the military and the government. The minority ethnic nationalities make up the remaining one-third, live mainly in the resource-rich border areas and hills of Burma, although many have been forcibly removed from their homes by the military-backed government, as it confiscated land for development projects and resource exploitation. As a result, millions of people from these minority groups have become internally displaced people (IDPs) within Burma, or refugees in neighbouring countries.[9] The seven largest minorities are the Chin, the Kachin, the Karenni (sometimes called Kayah), the Karen (sometimes called Kayin), the Mon, the Rakhine and the Shan. Burma is divided into seven states, each named after these seven ethnic nationalities, and seven regions (formerly called divisions), which are largely inhabited by the Bamar (Burmans). Among the ethnic minorities, the Rohingyas' nationality is disputed and, therefore, the government does not recognize them as citizens of Burma. The international media projects their sufferings as one of the worst discrimination and human rights abuses of all the people of Myanmar. Estimates put the Rohingya population of Burma at close to two million, living mainly in Rakhine State, and many more live as refugees in neighbouring countries, like Bangladesh.[10] The relative position vis-à-vis Bamar people have led to the marginalization of these communities because their lack of initiative in forging a national identity as well as repetitive repression by successive military governments.

The ethnic differences and strongholds were promoted by Britishers in the past. On February 12, 1947, the Union of Burma was founded at Panglong by four former British colonies, namely Chinram, Kachin Hills, Federated Shan States and Burma Proper, all of which already had their own constitutions. The British had occupied these four colonies separately as independent countries in different periods of time and had applied different administrative systems in accordance with different constitutions that the colonial power had promulgated for them. The British officially promulgated the Chinram Constitution, called the 'Chin Hills Regulation', in 1896, the 'Kachin Hill Tribes Regulation' in 1895, the '1919 Act of Federated Shan States' in 1920 and the '1935 Burma Act' in 1937.[11] The Chin Hills Regulation of 1896 covered the present Chin state in Burma, present Mizoram state, Nagaland state, and parts of Manipur and Meghalaya states in India. The 1935 Burma Act was applied to the area of the pre-colonial Myanmar/Burman Kingdom, which included the former Arakan and Mon Kingdoms as well as delta areas of Karen country.[12]

At the Panglong Conference in 1947, the Chin, Kachin, Shan and other non-Burman nationalities were promised the right to exercise political authority (in the form of administrative, judicial and legislative powers in their own autonomous national states) and to preserve and protect their language, culture and religion in exchange for voluntarily joining the Burmans in forming a political union and giving their loyalty to a new state. On the basis of the Panglong Agreement, the Union Constitution was framed. Aung San himself drafted the Union Constitution and submitted it to the Anti-Fascist People's Freedom League (AFPFL) convention held in May 1947 at the Jubilee Hall in Rangoon. Aung San delivered a long speech at the convention and explained the essence of the Panglong Agreement, which had the aim of establishing a Federal Union. Aung San also insisted on the right of self-determination for ethnic nationalities, who signed the Panglong Agreement to found a new Federal Union with so-called Burma Proper. He referred to his co-signatories, the Chin, Kachin and Shan, as nations, or *pyidaung* in Burmese.[13] However, lack of application of these promises created wide differences in perceptions about the agreement.

As a result, the ethnic fissures in the country started within months of independence, when Myanmar (then known as Burma) was torn apart by ethnic rebellion. For the rest of the period down to the 1962 coup, ethnic issues were so pressing that army leaders used them to justify their power grab. Under successive authoritarian regimes, nationalism has remained a central feature of the political landscape. For six decades of this sovereign state, the political agenda has thus been dominated by problems of democratization and nationalist conflict.[14] Right since 1962, when General Ne Win seized power from Prime Minister U Nu, Ne Win instituted the 'Burmese Way to Socialism', which systematically impoverished the country that had 90 per cent literacy rate and was rich in natural resources.[15] Ne Win's regime spent decades engaged in military operations against the Communist Party of Burma and various ethnic minorities fighting for autonomy or independence from the central government, which has traditionally been dominated by ethnic Burmans. Even under the rule of the British Empire, however, Burma was never a unified political state, but rather an agglomeration of many ethnic groups with little in common. The British allowed the ethnic areas in upper Burma to retain their social structures, including a degree of self-governance, while ruling lower Burma with professional civil service corps. The military government changed the country's name from Burma to Myanmar in 1989.[16]

For nearly four decades, the military government tried to assimilate the ethnic minorities, but given the intrinsic structure of self-governance, it led to contest between the military Junta and the ethnic minorities. In 1996, the State Peace and Development Council

(SPDC) escalated military operations in an effort to eliminate all remaining armed opposition by ethnic groups. Later, despite the regime having signed cease fire agreements with many ethnic leaders, the protests continued, thereby fuelling the exodus of refugees and displaced persons.[17] The national assimilation was also affected by the religious affiliation albeit to a very limited extent because even Karen minority does have a Karen Buddhist Army seeking nationhood.

An important angle to the lack of ethnic minority assimilation was the predominance of Buddhism in Myanmar's political set up. In the country, traditionally, Buddhist monks and institutions legitimized political authority, with person's power being justified and based on one's past ethical action (*Karma*). Hence, the political power was always accorded religious legitimacy, and the subjects (the people) accepting the person in authority as being sanctioned by Buddhism was thus seen as just and right. After independence, Buddhism increasingly became identified with nationalism, national identity and integrity. Burmese Buddhism has a long tradition of being the rallying point for resistance against unjust power, be it colonialists or military junta, and this facilitated the emergence of the *Sangha* (Buddhist Monkhood), as a major political force.[18] The monk resistance movement in 2007 broke the sanctity of the military junta rule, which led to subtle liberalization of governance in Myanmar.

The 2007 Saffron Revolution triggered the need for talks between the government and the ethnic minorities. One important aspect of differences with ethnic minorities was the lack of their role in the country's constitution and the devolution of power from centralized administration to decentralized empowerment of provinces. At the final session of the National Convention on 18 July 2007, the Kachin Independence Organization (KIO) delegates, a prominent ethnic community, put up 19 points that were endorsed by the other nationalities to be included in the constitution. However, all of them were rejected.[19] In 2008, Myanmar's ruling State Peace and Development Council (SPDC) announced that a referendum on the final draft of the country's new constitution would be organized, followed by multi-party elections in 2010. Reacting to international pressure to include Aung San Suu Kyi and the National League for Democracy (NLD) in a belated broadening of the country's political process before the referendum, the military regime, headed by Senior General Than Shwe, made it clear that it would pursue its roadmap to a "disciplined" democracy as planned.[20] Since then, Myanmar has progressed, even though incrementally in terms of electoral reforms, media freedom, liberal economic policies and even initiating concrete talks with estranged ethnic minorities to assimilate them in nation building. In most of the discourses, this incremental progress has been cautiously lauded, but at times criticized. Anyhow, the international decision makers have shown the intent to lift sanctions from the reclusive regime, highlighting the positive feedback on the developments in the country. It is not that the state has not made any attempts for ethnic assimilation; efforts were taken right since independence.

State's Efforts towards National Reconciliation

The Burmese government has had contentious relationships with its ethnic minority groups, which account for about one-third of the country's more than 54 million inhabitants, and many have fought for greater autonomy or secession for their regions since the country gained independence from Great Britain in 1948. Even before independence, in 1947, General Aung San, the young military leader, who quickly became the hero of the Burmese independence movement, met with leaders of the country's various ethnic minorities in the Shan town of Panglong to discuss their status within a soon-to-be independent Burma. Their meeting concluded with the signing of the Panglong Agreement, an accord that was to pave the way for a new constitution and, eventually, independence. Over 60 years later, the promises of the Panglong Agreement remain unfulfilled and ethnic conflict continued to plague the nation, but the elusive 'spirit' of Panglong still affects the Burmese of every ethnicity.[21]

In 2011, leaders of the United Nationalities Federal Council (UNFC), an umbrella group comprised of 11 of Myanmar's leading ethnic groups, including the Mon, Shan, Karenni, Chin and Kachin people, released a statement announcing that they were prepared to meet with Myanmar's chief negotiator, U Aung Min Aung Min, to present their version of a durable roadmap to peace. At the end of 2011, the government launched peace initiatives with several of Myanmar's ethnic armies.[22] Reformist President Thein Sein has signed cease-fire agreements with most of Myanmar's armed ethnic groups since he came to power in 2011, and signed a temporary peace agreement at the end of May 2011 with the Kachin in a bid to end the country's last major ethnic conflict. The Kachin and other ethnic groups have called for greater autonomy and increased representation in the president's nominally civilian government, which has set Myanmar on a path to democracy after decades of military misrule.[23]

Since taking office in March 2011, President Thein Sein of Myanmar took important steps to improve the prospects for peace between the government (dominated by Myanmar's ethnic majority, the Bamar) and the country's ethnic minorities. A staggering 12 ceasefires have been signed with ethnic armed groups in 2011 alone.[24] Viewed as key to the development of Myanmar, the suspension of EU sanctions announced on April 23, 2012, was seen as another major endorsement of President U Thein Sein's political reforms, which included the release of hundreds of political prisoners, new laws allowing labour unions and strikes, a gradual easing of media restrictions, and ceasefire agreements with various ethnic rebel groups.[25] However, problems amassed during five decades of military misrule have proved resistant to rapid resolution of various conflicts. National reconciliation with ethnic groups has still not materialized in the Kachin state, and was severely damaged by violence in Rakhine state.[26]

Subsequently, more than a dozen ethnic groups with a loose alliance in June 2013 decided to establish a unified political party in a bid to secure greater representation for Myanmar's minorities in the National Parliament ahead of 2015 elections. The agreement by 15 of the groups to form the Federated Union Party (FUP) was made on the opening day of a two-day conference held in eastern Myanmar's Shan state capital of Taunggyi, according to Oo Hla Saw, General Secretary of the Rakhine Nationality Development Party

(RNDP).[27] The FUP will consist of 15 political groups from the Nationalities Brotherhood Federation (NBF)—an ethnic alliance initially formed from the RNDP, Shan Nationalities Democratic Party (SNDP), Chin National Party, All Mon Regions Democracy Party and Phalon-Sawal Democratic Party after Myanmar's 2010 by-election.[28] Meanwhile, Myanmar's civilian government has reached a peace deal with the ethnic Wa guerrilla group as a part of an effort to reach agreements with all the ethnic groups in the country. Earlier, the Wa region was singled out by the international community for its involvement in huge drug problems in the region. BBC reported that a delegation was sent to the remote Wa region in Shan state, which borders China, to hold talks on the peace deal with United Wa State Army (UWSA), which is believed to be the largest fighting force with as many as 30,000 rebels. According to the report, the country's military and the UWSA have agreed to hold regular meetings and withdraw their positions that they had occupied before a recent stand-off. The UWSA is said to be equipped with state-of-the-art weaponry. China reportedly supplied combat helicopters to the group.[29] With positive responses and the need for development, the peace between the Myanmar government and the ethnic rebels is likely to be long lasting, however, the incidents of attacks on Rohingyas, followed by attacks on Muslims in Central Myanmar and the resultant international condemnation would have an effect on the nation building process.

International Responses to Attack on Rohingyas

Rohingyas are the people residing in the Arakan province of Myanmar. In recent decades, this ethnic and religious minority has been stripped of its citizenship and property rights by Myanmar's military-dominated government, leading to human rights abuses and exploitation and resulting in mass exodus. It is estimated that some 200,000 Rohingyas have fled to Bangladesh over the years, with smaller numbers fleeing to Indonesia, Malaysia, Thailand and elsewhere in the region by boat.[30] Rohingyas are a religious and linguistic ethnic minority from Burma's northern Rakhine state, who have been facing state-sponsored persecution in their homeland since

1978. In 1991, when the population experienced widespread repression and abuse from security forces posted in Rakhine, a quarter of a million crossed the border to Bangladesh seeking asylum. Most of them still live there today. Some 28,000 have been officially recognized as refugees and are living in UN run camps, waiting to be relocated to a third nation. Hundreds of thousands of others live outside UN run camps in the district of Chittagong or in unofficial camps, stateless and hopeless.[31] According to the UNHCR, there are around 1,800 Rohingya registered as asylum seekers in India. Each one has been issued an identity card to protect them from harassment, arbitrary arrest, detention and expulsion, and to prevent them from being forced back to a country where their life or freedom may be in danger.[32] The Rohingyas are indigenous people of Arakan with a distinct culture, language (a unique mixture of Bengali, Urdu and Arakanese), civilization and religion of their own. Through commercial shipping activity in the Bay of Bengal, a small Muslim settlement was established in Arakan, an independent state at that time. However, when the Burmese conquered Arakan and annexed it in 1785, the Muslims in Arakan became a minority in a predominantly Buddhist environment.[33] The Muslim community increased slowly through marriage, natural increase, conversion and a growth in the number of traders and adventurers. Although these Burmese Muslims (known as Rohingyas) were looked upon as different, they were tolerated as they were loyal to the king, inactive as a small community and posed no threat to the Buddhist population. The bulk of the Muslims arrived in Myanmar during the 125 years of British rule, from the time of the first Anglo-Burmese war. The defeat by the British forced Myanmar to sign the Treaty of Yandabo in 1826, which resulted in the absorption of Arakan and Tenasserim into the British Empire. While poor communication and natural barriers isolated Arakan from the rest of Myanmar, the border between Chittagong and Arakan was porous since British rule spanned both Myanmar and Bengal. The settlements of Bengali Muslims (known as Chittagongs) moved into Northern Arakan and began to merge with the Rohingya community. Over time, the distinction between the two ethnic groups was blurred due to constant cross-border interactions.[34]

In Myanmar, Buddhists are proud of their ethnic identity and religion. Besides ignoring demands for recognition of their unique ethnic and religious identity, the state government has persisted in denying the Rohingyas their basic human rights. In Myanmar, the Rohingyas have no legal status and are usually stateless. In February 1992, the Minister of Foreign Affairs, U Ohn Gyaw claimed that:

> ... although there are 135 national races living in Myanmar today, the so-called Rohingya people are not one of them.
>
> Historically there has never been a Rohingya race in Myanmar... people of the Muslim faith from the adjacent country illegally entered Myanmar Naing Ngan, particularly Rakhine state.[35]

According to the 1982 citizenship law, they qualify only for associate citizenship or naturalized citizenship. Rohingyas are issued white identity cards instead of the red ones issued to citizens of Myanmar. Having a white identity card was an official declaration that the Rohingyas were 'foreign residents' within the country. "Since they are seen as illegal immigrants, this has allowed the State Law and Order Restoration Council (SLORC rechristened later as State Peace and Development Council, SPDC) government to justify its actions, such as denying the people their fundamental rights and subjecting them to innumerable hardships. According to the refugees interviewed, the SLORC government has also begun a policy to move non-Muslim Burmese into Northern Arakan to displace the Rohingyas. Mosques were locked up and destroyed, with Buddhist temples being erected in their place. Land was confiscated for military use or distributed to non-Muslims for housing projects using Muslim labour. The Muslims were often persecuted because of their religious practices. Under the pretence of eliminating the alarming rate of 'illegal' entry, the government unleashed Operation Nagmin (Dragon King) in 1978. The harassment, arrests and brute force the Rohingyas were subjected to led to an exodus of about 200,000 refugees into Bangladesh. However, negotiations between Bangladesh and

Myanmar resulted in the repatriation of 187,250 refugees to Arakan by December 29 1979." The influx of refugees did not stop, and in 1992, about 250,000 refugees crossed into Bangladesh to seek asylum from the government's extra-judicial killings, execution, arrests, torture, restriction on movements, slave labour, forced eviction of residents, confiscation of lands, desecration of mosques and the rape of women. Forced portering and slave labour were clearly documented in a report by the Amnesty International in May 1992. By conducting interviews with the Muslim refugees from Maungdaw and Buthidaung, the extent of the problem was highlighted. The soldiers did not allow the people to remove the dead bodies and thus the dead were frequently left by the tracks unless their relatives secretly buried them.[36]

Speaking before the US Senate Committee on Foreign Relations Subcommittee on East Asian and Pacific Affairs on 26 April, Joseph Yun, Principal Deputy Assistant Secretary, Bureau of East Asian and Pacific Affairs of the US State Department, noted: "In Rakhine State, systematic discrimination and denial of human rights against ethnic Rohingya remains deplorable. Overall, the legacy of five decades of military rule—repressive laws, a pervasive security apparatus, a corrupt judiciary and media censorship—is all too present."[37] However, the role of many of West Asian nations was primarily to project their image as the protector of minority rights (primarily Muslims) all across the world. This started with the statements by Iran, followed by those of Turkey and Saudi Arabia. Turkey minister also visited Myanmar along with a few of the OIC members to assess the situation on the ground. Later, the resolution and statements were released after the OIC meeting in Jeddah,[38] which made special mention of the plight of Rohingyas in Myanmar. Iran taking note of developments, especially ethno-religious clashes interacted with the Myanmar government and requested the Myanmar government to stem the ethnic riots. While Myanmar government refused to allow OIC to open a liaison office in the country (ostensibly as a result of Monks' protest on the issue), however, it permitted Iran to start an inter-faith dialogue in Myanmar to resolve the ethno-religious tension in the country. Each nation has been trying to highlight Rohingyas issues to its own benefit, without comprehensively looking at the problem. This has resulted in the rise of Buddhist nationalism. This might trigger unrest and inter-religious conflict. Myanmar needs time for addressing these problems, but at its own pace.

Conclusion

Myanmar's road to democracy appears promising and it becomes imperative for the nation to assimilate its ethnic minorities. The military rule of all these years have failed to build a nation even though it was successful in keeping the ethnic minorities in one fold through occasional concessions and ceasefire agreements. Therefore, with the formation of unified peace organizations and consultative committees among the ethnic minority parties along with participation in provincial legislature as well as administration has opened new avenues for peace making and nation building. However, the terms and mode of assimilation of ethnic minorities should be surgical and must be done as per the institutional set-up within Myanmar. Given the fact that any ethnic assimilation would demand an equal share in duties and responsibilities, any laggardness or deficit in commitment to the cause would further alienate the ethnic minorities. The ethnic minorities must also understand that the new deluge of investment and growth opportunities would give them succour from poverty and hunger. In this process, the interference from the outside agencies and power should be kept at bare minimum.

REFERENCES

1. Khin Zaw Win. 2010 and the Unfinished Task of Nation Building, in Nick Cheesman, Monique Skidmore and Trevor Wilson (eds.). *Ruling Myanmar: From Cyclone Nargis to National Elections* (Singapore: ISEAS, 2010), p. 21.
2. Anthony D. Smith. *Nations and Nationalism in a Global Era* (Cambridge: Polity Press, 1995), pp. 56-57 quoted in Khin Zaw Win, *Op. Cit.*, 2010, p. 19.
3. Dr. Wan Norhasniah Wan Husin. Nation-Building and 1 Malaysia Concept: Ethnic Relations Challenges In The Educational Field, *International Journal of Humanities and Social Science*, vol. 1, no. 9 [Special Issue—July 2011], pp. 228-229.

Also see J. Hippler. *Ethnicity, State and Nation-Building: Experience Policies and Conceptualization*, Ausafze, 2002, pp. 1-5.

4. Jochen Hippler. "Problems of Democracy and Nation Building in Pakistan" http://www.jochenhippler.de/html/problems_of_democracy_and_nation-building_in_pakistan.html (Accessed July 15, 2013).
5. Dr. Wan Norhasniah Wan Husin. Nation-Building and 1 Malaysia Concept: Ethnic Relations Challenges in the Educational Field, *International Journal of Humanities and Social Science*, vol. 1, no. 9 [Special Issue — July 2011].
6. Burma detains monk who led 2007 Saffron uprising at http://www.telegraph.co.uk/news/worldnews/asia/burmamyanmar/9074364/Burma-detains-monk-who-led-2007-Saffron-uprising.html/ (Accessed June 25, 2013).
7. Ian Holliday. Voting and Violence in Myanmar: Nation Building for a Transition to Democracy, *Asian Survey*, vol. 48, no. 6 (November/December 2008), p. 1039.
8. Lian H. Sakhong. The Dynamics of Sixty Years of Ethnic Armed Conflict in Burma, Analysis Paper No. 1, January 2012, p. 1.
9. Ethnic Nationalities of Burma. http://www.oxfordburmaalliance.org/ethnic-groups.html (Accessed June 25, 2013). Also see Excluded: Burma's Ethnic Nationalities on the Margins of Development and Democracy, Community Organizing and Rights Education-Burma (CORE) at http://www.burmapartnership.org/2012/12/excluded/ (Accessed June 25, 2013).
10. Ethnic Nationalities of Burma at http://www.oxfordburmaalliance.org/ethnic-groups.html (Accessed June 25, 2013).
11. Lian H. Sakhong. A Struggle for Democracy, Equality and Federalism in Burma: An Ethnic Perspective in Johan Lagerkvist (ed.), '*Between Isolation and Internationalization: The State of Burma*' (Stockholm: The Swedish Institute of International Affairs, 2008).
12. *Ibid.*
13. Lian H. Sakhong. A Struggle for Democracy, Equality and Federalism in Burma: An Ethnic Perspective, at http://www.encburma.net/index.php/polocy-papers/37-policypapers/188-a-struggle-for-democracy-equality-and-federalism-in-burma-an-ethnic-perspective.html (Accessed June 25, 2013).
14. Ian Holliday. Voting and Violence in Myanmar: Nation Building for a Transition to Democracy, *Asian Survey*, vol. 48, no. 6 (November/December 2008), p. 1039.
15. Mathea Falco. Burma: Time for Change, Council on Foreign Relations, New York, 2003, p. 7.
16. *Ibid.*, pp. 7-8.
17. *Ibid.*, p. 30.
18. Bilveer Singh. Religion as a Political Ideology in Southeast Asia, in Ishtiaq

Ahmed (ed.). *The Politics of Religion in South and Southeast Asia* (New York: Routledge, 2011), p. 130.

19. Khin Zaw Win, *Op. Cit.*, 2010, p. 23.
20. Jurgen Hacke. ASEAN and Political Change in Myanmar: Towards a Regional Initiative, *Contemporary Southeast Asia*, vol. 30, no. 3 (2008), p. 351.
21. Matthew J. Walton. Ethnicity, Conflict, and History in Burma: The Myths of Panglong, *Asian Survey*, vol. 48, no. 6 (November/December 2008), p. 889.
22. Myanmar: Ethnic minorities call for caution as sanctions ease at http://www.irinnews.org/report/95370/myanmar-ethnic-minorities-call-for-caution-as-sanctions-ease (Accessed June 25, 2013).
23. Fifteen Myanmar Ethnic Groups to Form Unified Party at http://www.rfa.org/english/news/myanmar/party-06112013190735.html (Accessed June 25, 2013)
24. Christianna Gozzi. Myanmar: Bridging Narratives, October 9, 2012 at http://ac4.ei.columbia.edu/2012/10/09/myanmar-bridging-narratives/(Accessed June 25, 2013).
25. Myanmar: Ethnic minorities call for caution as sanctions ease at http://www.irinnews.org/report/95370/myanmar-ethnic-minorities-call-for-caution-as-sanctions-ease (Accessed June 25, 2013).
26. Ian Holliday. Myanmar in 2012: Toward a Normal State, *Asian Survey*, vol. 53, no. 1 (February 2013), p. 93.
27. Fifteen Myanmar Ethnic Groups to Form Unified Party at http://www.rfa.org/english/news/myanmar/party-06112013190735.html (Accessed June 25, 2013).
28. *Ibid.*
29. Myanmar enters peace agreement with Wa guerrilla group, July 14, 2012. http://www.business-standard.com/article/news-ani/myanmar-enters-peace-agreement-with-wa-guerrilla-group-113071400349_1.html (Accessed May 2, 2012).
30. Myanmar: Rohingyas in Malaysia seek education, opportunities. http://www.irinnews.org/Report/92933/MYANMAR-Rohingyas-in-Malaysia-seek-education-opportunities (Accessed May 2, 2012). Also see Pankaj Jha, Rohingyas Refugees: Addressing a Regional Problem having International Ramifications, *International Journal of Social Science —ARIDSS*, vol. 1, no. 1 (January -December 2011), pp. 39-50.
31. Pankaj Jha, Rohingyas Refugees: Addressing a Regional Problem having International Ramifications, *International Journal of Social Science—ARIDSS*, Vol. 1, No. 1 (January -December 2011), pp. 39-50. Also see Misha Hussain and Kutu Palong. For Rohingya in Bangladesh, No Place is Home, Feb. 19, 2010. http://www.time.com/time/world/article/0, 8599, 1966621, 00.html (Accessed May 2, 2012).

32. Zarni Mann. Rohingyas in India Demand Full Refugee Status, The Irrawaddy, May 1, 2012. http://www.irrawaddy.org/archives/3388 (Accessed May 2, 2012). Also see Pankaj Jha, *Op. Cit.*, 2011.

33. Carl Grundy-Warr, Ananda Rajah, Elaine Wong Siew Yin, and Zulkifli Ali. 'Power, Territoriality and Cross Border Insecurity: Regime Security as an Aspect of Burma's Refugee Crisis', *Geopolitics*, (1997) Vol. 2, No. 2, pp. 101-102. Also see Pankaj Jha, *Op. Cit.*, 2011, pp. 39-50.

33. Carl Grundy-Warr, *Ibid.*, p. 102

34. Carl Grundy-Warr, *Ibid.* Also see Pankaj Jha, *Op. Cit.*, 2011.

35. Carl Grundy-Warr, Ananda Rajah, Elaine Wong Siew Yin, and Zulkifli Ali, *Op. Cit.*, 1997.

36. Grundy Warr, *Ibid*, pp. 102-103. Also see Pankaj Jha, *Op. Cit.*, 2011.

37. Myanmar: Ethnic minorities call for caution as sanctions ease. http://www.irinnews.org/report/95370/myanmar-ethnic-minorities-call-for-caution-as-sanctions-ease (Accessed June 25, 2013).

38. OIC conference on Rohingyas in Jeddah next week. http://www.arabnews.com/news/457095 (Accessed July 16, 2013).

SECTION II

Political Relations

5
Political Relations between Myanmar and India

Chaw Chaw Sein

This chapter on Political Relations between Myanmar and India has been divided into four parts: the geopolitical outlook of India; the security outlook of India; the geo-economic outlook of India and the future of India-Myanmar relations.

Geo-political Outlook of India

From past 60 years, India's relations with South Asia have been hegemonic in nature. India is the harbinger of stability in the chronically unstable South Asian region. Though India's relationship with Pakistan is evolving positively and the 'composite dialogue' launched in early 2004 has clearly decreased tension; however, India-Pakistan relations remains a central element of uncertainty. India's relationships with Nepal, Bangladesh and Sri Lanka are closely linked to the domestic situation in these countries, as they affect India's own security. The process of integration in the South Asian Association for Regional Cooperation (SAARC) is hampered by bilateral disputes. Still, it remains a potentially important framework of cooperation.

The India-EU relationship has been growing steadily since 1962 when diplomatic relations were established between India and the European Economic Communities. A regular political dialogue has been started between India and EU since the first Summit started in 2000. Since the 2004 Summit, India-EU relationship took the shape of a Strategic Partnership, making India one of the EU's carefully selected main global partners. The wide-ranging Joint Action Plan—to implement the Strategic Partnership in all areas from political, trade and economic to cultural, civil society and development issues—agreed upon at the 6th Summit in 2005, further boosted relations.

India has increasingly asserted itself on the international stage, seeking greater presence in multilateral institutions, for example, through its campaign for a permanent seat in the UN Security Council. India shares its commitment to a multi-polar world system with Russia and China, with whom it shares a common vision on many international issues, such as non-interference in domestic affairs. The traditional close friendship with Russia is maintained, and relations with China are growing politically and economically. India is implementing its 'Look East' policy, underpinned by economic considerations, towards its eastern neighbours in ASEAN, of which India is a full dialogue partner.

India's relationship with the United States has developed strongly since the late 1990s, despite America's good relations with Pakistan. A regular political and strategic dialogue with the US on bilateral and regional issues is a new feature of India's foreign policy. Defence and security cooperation programmes with the US are on the increase. The US-India Summit of July 2005 attracted strong international attention, notably through their agreement to boost civil nuclear cooperation.

Security Outlook of India

The Indian Ocean is home to many choke points, such as the Strait of Hormuz, Malacca and Sunda Straits. India perceives China's partnership with Pakistan as part of a broader Chinese strategy to expand its influence in South Asia. China has already been probing its westward boundaries, reasserting its territorial claims against India in Aksai Chin and Arunachal Pradesh, and its navy is developing blue-water capabilities, which could challenge Indian interests in the Indian Ocean. India is particularly alarmed by the recent docking of Chinese naval ships in Myanmar, and by China's role in developing the Pakistani deep-water port in Gwadar.

Since most of the trade of the Indian Ocean littorals and the South Asian states is seaborne, SLOCs form the lifeline of these countries. According to World Bank estimates, in 1999 the world seaborne trade was pegged at 21,480 billion ton-miles; which is expected to reach 35,000 billion ton-miles in 2010 and 41,800 billion ton-miles in 2014. As oceans face a number of threats, including piracy, maritime terrorism, drug trafficking, gun-running, human smuggling, pollution, accidents and inter-state conflicts, these threats are likely to see a proportional rise.

While the best approach to SLOC security lies in extensive cooperation, the fact is that SLOCs arouse different response strategies amongst different people. To a military analyst, the SLOCs are related to the maritime instruments of power, and maritime geography becomes the pivot on which forces must be deployed. To a politician, on the other hand, SLOCs signify the state of relations with countries located along the sea routes, while for an economist SLOCs is just the shortest and most economical travel distance between two destinations. Over the last decade or so, India has developed good security relationships with many states throughout the Indian Ocean.

The Southwest Indian Ocean forms the gateway between the Atlantic and Indian Oceans. India's security relationships in the region are anchored by its close relationship with Mauritius. India has long-standing and close political, economic and security associations with Mauritius. Some 70 per cent of the Mauritian population is of Indian ethnic origin and for several decades, Mauritius has acted as the primary gateway for international investment into India. Since 2003, the Indian Navy has provided maritime security through periodic patrols of Mauritian waters including anti-piracy patrols in 2010. India is also growing security relationships with Madagascar, Mozambique and the Seychelles. It has provided two helicopters and training to the Seychelles security forces.

India is also developing security relations in the Northwest India Ocean particularly with Qatar and Oman. The Indian Navy has sought to play an active role in Somali-based piracy. A security agreement was formalized that will significantly enhance India's capabilities in the central Indian Ocean. India has been granted use of the former British naval and air base on Gan Island, part of the southernmost group of islands in the Maldives. Northeast Indian Ocean, which encompasses the Straits of Malacca and large portions of the South China Sea, is of concern to both India and Myanmar. The Andaman Islands have particular significance for the security of the Straits.

Geo-economic Outlook of India

India's geo-economic outlook focuses on Southeast Asia (Look East policy), Africa (West Bound Strategy) and Central Asia (Look North Policy). Central Asia has become important for India because of the discovery of hydrocarbon reserves and as it has become a major transportation hub for gas and oil pipelines, multi-modal communication corridors connecting China, Russia, Europe, the Caucasus region, the Trans-Caspian region and the Indian Ocean. Central Asia and South Asia are intimately connected not only geographically, but also strategically. Security and economic issues are the two most important components of the Central Asian states' engagement with outside powers.

Myanmar-India Relations and Future Prospect

Having geographical, historical and cultural affinity, common experiences of colonial rule and common policy of peaceful co-existence and mutual cooperation, the relations between Myanmar and India (1948-1962) under Premier U Nu and Prime Minister Nehru were not only cordial, but also very close. However, when General Ne Win came to power in March 1962, the relations between Myanmar and India cooled down.

During 1962 to 1988, political relations between Myanmar and India were affected due to the Enterprise Nationalization Law, which hit the interest of Indian businessmen in Myanmar. There were some serious problems, such as Naga and Mizo insurgent problems, Sino-India border dispute and India's shifting policy from non-interference and non-alignment. Although the relationship between Myanmar and India was not as warm as previously, the two governments endeavoured to re-establish warm relations with mutual pursuit of non-alignment and mutual understanding.

However, India's clear stand on the democracy movement in 1988 was one of the factors, which had negative impact on the relations between Myanmar and India. As India is a vibrant democracy, India denounced the presence of an undemocratic government in Myanmar. While maintaining its policy of strict non-interference in the internal affairs of Myanmar, India continued its principle support to the democratic aspirations of the people of Myanmar. While supporting a resolution critical of Myanmar in the third Committee of the United Nations, the Government of India also expressed its concern about the absence of democracy and widespread infringement of human rights in Myanmar. India's criticism of the SLORC government in international forum and its expression of support for pro-democratic activists of Myanmar during 1990-1991 led to unfriendly relationship between the two countries.

However, India shifted its policy on Myanmar after 1992 for four reasons. The growing triangular relationship between China, Pakistan and Myanmar, concerned India, because the increasing strategic linkages between Myanmar and China was against India's interests, as China-Pakistan's alliance on the western front was a cause of concern for India. Indian government firmly believed that there were supplies of conventional weapons from Pakistan to Myanmar, the training of army personnel in Pakistan and China's support of arms and training to India's ethnic insurgents from Nagaland, Mizoram and Manipur.

In that context, China had engaged in assisting Pakistan, both in terms of equipment as well as finance, to build a major port at Gwadar near the Pakistan-Iran border. China had also financed the building of US$ 248 million port, which could help boost Pakistan's naval capability as well as provide China with a support location near the strategically located oil-rich region of the Persian Gulf. Indian Ocean is important for China's oil imports from the Gulf as well as its European trade. Therefore, China's strategic plans in the naval field raised the concerns in both Southeast Asian countries as well as India. Furthermore, China has helped in building up the capacity of Myanmar's armed forces as well as infrastructure development following sanctions from Western countries. Since 1988, China had officially been Myanmar's main supplier of armaments, military technology and aid, whereas, India refused to sell weapons to the Government of Myanmar for 15 years.

As the economic development in China is concentrated on the coastal region, China was looking for a shorter access to the sea for its economically backward southern provinces of Yunnan, Sichuan and Guangxi. The short land route to the Indian Ocean for China's isolated and economically backward Southern provinces through Myanmar was the most economical and easier for China. Nevertheless, China's access to Myanmar's Coco Island, north of Andaman Islands of India and a naval radar system at Myanmar's Zadetkyi Island have become a major cause of concern for India.

Another factor of Indian policy shift concerns with its Northeast Region. The mounting problem of insurgency coupled with the menace of arm-trafficking in India's Northeast region propelled India to change its approach from that of confrontation to a cautious engagement with the SLORC government. Improved relationship with Myanmar is essential for India as it is the land bridge between India's North-east region and ASEAN countries. The development of the North-east region is very important political, economic and social issue for India. The North-east region, sandwiched between Bangladesh, Bhutan, Tibet and Myanmar, accounts for 98 per cent of its borders with these four countries. Though, the natural, shortest and easiest access for the North-east region of India to the rest of India lies across Bangladesh, but, Bangladesh has not given transit rights to India.

As Bangladesh has not shown any willingness to cooperate with India, the only other outlet for the North-east region is through Myanmar. Therefore, Myanmar remains not only an area of security interest, but also for economic development of India's North-east region.

The Government of India had adopted two most pragmatic policies, such as the 'Look East Policy' (LEP) and 'Constructive Engagement' with Myanmar. Prime Minister P.V. Narasimha Rao initiated the LEP, by which the India-Myanmar relations came into focus. Rao reversed India's policies towards Myanmar and put initiatives to rebuild a viable relationship. Myanmar remains an area of security interest for India not only on account of the activities of the north-east insurgents groups that set up camps across the Indian border, but also the activities of countries working against India's legitimate security concerns.

India's efforts to improve relations with ASEAN, was an important factor in improving relations with the government of Myanmar. Geo-politically, with friendly relations with Myanmar, India could instil more substance to its LEP of building relationships with Southeast Asia, as Myanmar bridges South Asia and India with South-east Asia. Myanmar is a crucial factor in the security and stability of the region, as internal and external developments in Myanmar have direct and considerable effect on the vital national interests of India as well as South-east Asian countries. As Myanmar has considerable energy resources, energy is another factor for India's interests in Myanmar.

In 2011, Myanmar was at the stage of seventh step of the roadmap to democracy to build a new modern, developed and democratic nation with a new constitution. The new government of the Republic of the Union of Myanmar was established on 31 March 2011. At the invitation of the President of India, Smt. Pratibha Devisingh Patil, President of the Republic of the Union of Myanmar, U Thein Sein paid a state visit to India on 12 October, 2011. This was the first state visit to India following the swearing of a new Government in Myanmar in March 2011 that marked welcome progress in moving towards an open and democratic framework. The Prime Minister of India, Dr. Manmohan Singh congratulated the President of Myanmar on the transition towards democratic government and offered all necessary assistance in strengthening the democratic transition in an inclusive and broad based manner. He also welcomed the ongoing efforts at political, economic and social reforms in Myanmar. The President of Myanmar and the Prime Minister of India reiterated their shared commitment to strengthen and broaden the multifaceted relationship based on shared history, civilizational ties and close religious, linguistic and cultural affinities, and take it to a new level. The impetus provided by high level discussions has contributed in enhancing bilateral economic cooperation and possess a huge potential for the expansion of trade.

A historic milestone in the relations between Myanmar and India was the visit of the Prime Minister of the Republic of India, Dr. Manmohan Singh from 27 to 29 May 2012. This was the first visit by an Indian Prime Minister to Myanmar after 25 years. During the visit, Dr. Manmohan Singh insisted that Myanmar is a critical partner in India's LEP and is perfectly situated to play the role of an economic bridge between India and China and between South and South-east Asia. The visit showed that the political relations between Myanmar and India were very close and cordial.

The increased momentum of bilateral visits and interactions is a positive contributing factor to strengthen close and friendly relations between Myanmar and India. These frequent exchanges of visits have proved as instruments to further develop and strengthen the multi-dimensional relationship in the areas of security, trade and economic cooperation as well as social interactions between the two countries.

For India, good relations with its neighbours are central to its foreign policy. Myanmar is geo-strategically important for India. The specific objective of building substantive co-operation and engagement between Myanmar and India are to create cooperative arrangements between the two countries to counter secessionist and terrorist activities in the border areas. The second objective is to enhance mutual cooperation in controlling the illegal trafficking of drugs from the Golden Triangle across sub-continental India to other parts of the world. Moreover, China's South-east Asian policies have become a major factor, which has influenced India's policies towards the ASEAN region, especially towards Myanmar. China is developing communication networks in the South-east Asian regions, participating in the construction of several trans-Asian roads and railway projects in collaboration with Myanmar, Thailand, Cambodia, Laos and Vietnam under the umbrella of the six-nation Greater Mekong Sub-Regional cooperation arrangement. Therefore, India's regional foreign policy orientations necessarily involve sustaining a relationship with Southeast Asian countries.

Being geographically the most proximate in South-east Asian country, Myanmar has a high priority in India's regional policies. The North-eastern states of India provide the bridge for connectivity to

Myanmar and other ASEAN countries. Myanmar is pivotal to India's LEP; therefore, India looks forward to building an enduring partnership of friendship, cooperation and common prosperity with Myanmar. Bilateral trade and development partnerships are the main areas guiding the relations between Myanmar and India. A number of projects are under implementation between the two countries including the Kaladan Multi-modal Transport Connectivity Project, Trilateral Highway Project, upgrading of Rhi-Tiddim and Rhi-Falam Roads and the Tamanthi Hydro Electric Project.

Conclusion

As for Myanmar, maintaining good-neighbourly relations with neighbouring countries is very important for its independence and active foreign policy. It highlights the importance of neighbouring countries in deepening Myanmar's ties with India. Myanmar is geographically situated between two highly populous nations, India and China. Improved relationship with India will provide peace and prosperity for Myanmar. As India is a growing potential power in the region, close and cordial relations with India is very important for Myanmar's long-term national interests and geo-political reality of its security interests. The traditional ties of friendly relations between Myanmar and India have been further strengthened by Myanmar's policy of maintaining friendly relations with neighbouring country and India's LEP. While the Government of India welcomed the political reconciliation and greater openness of Myanmar; the government of Myanmar has promulgated to adhere to the independent and active foreign policy. In line with its policy of constructive engagement, the Government of India has become aware of the importance of establishing a dialogue with its neighbouring country, Myanmar. As Myanmar is strategically important for India, it is imperative for India to engage with Myanmar politically, economically and militarily as well.

6

India-Myanmar: Rebuilding Synergies and Strengthening Partnership

Sonu Trivedi

The common frontiers and strong traditional ties between India and Myanmar have led to the emergence of closer relations between the two countries, which is based on mutual faith and kinship going beyond the ties of friendship. To quote General Aung San "Above all... we stand for more than friendly relations with our neighbours. We want to be not merely good neighbours, but good brothers."[1] This association and bonding based on the feeling of brotherhood between the two countries of India and Myanmar have guided our policies towards each other. In spite of the strains and misgivings that the two countries had for a brief period during the military rule and reallocation in their attitude during the decade of 1980s and 1990s, both countries have remained as brothers in a common family overcoming all adversities and treating each other sincerely. It is in this background of shared histories and geographical ties that this chapter explores India-Myanmar bilateral political relations. But any understanding of the contemporary political relations between the two countries remains incomplete without a peep into the rich cultural heritage and the past, which the two countries share. In this context, the first part of the chapter studies the historical legacy of the two countries and the need for rebuilding synergies. The realist consideration and pragmatism has been the main focus of the second part of the chapter, which further explores the factors guiding India's Myanmar policy. Strengthening partnership, re-engagement with the new regime, and the emerging challenges in the India-Myanmar relations is the subject matter of the concluding section.

The Legacy

The indelible mark of the Indian cultural influence on Burmese history is remarkable and worth studying. Its geographical proximity, long-time administrative union with India and our common struggle for freedom from colonial domination has further cemented our historic bonds. Historically, like other parts of South-east Asia, Burma came under the spell of Indian cultural influences (Suryanarayan 2009). Burmese legends indicate Indian contact from pre-historic days (Majumdar 1955). According to historian R.L. Soni (1955), "Burma and all her neighbours, whether in far east or north or south were under the sphere of influence of the great 'Greater India' cultural expansion". British historian Harvey in his book 'Outline of Burmese History' writes—"Although, Burmese are the outcome of Mongolian tribe, but their culture is far apart from them... Rather it resembles Indian culture" (1947). Legends and epics in India and Myanmar suggest that contacts between them go back to pre-historic times. References to 'Brahmadesh' and 'Swarnabhumi' abound our mythology and history (Bhaskar 2000: 356).

The amazing zeal of the early Buddhists of India laid an abiding foundation for cultural association between India and Myanmar. The Anawratha Dynasty (1044-1287) built many magnificent temples and religious structures, which represented a unique combination of Hindu and Burmese architecture (Chakravarti 1971: 3). It is surprising to know that the Burmese Buddhist law was derived from the laws of *'Manu'*. Buddhist religious texts and canons are written in *Pali,* which was the common language in India during 500 BC. Even, the Burmese script is based on the ancient Indian script—*Brahmi.* There are a number of phrases, several names and words suggestive of intimate Indian connection. As a result of arrival of Indians in Myanmar, there began a tradition of naming Burmese places with Sanskrit and Pali names, such as 'Pegu' was called *Usha.* Burmese name for the epic 'Ramayana' is *Yamayana.* The epic is still played all over Myanmar regularly. Religious structures having the images of Indian gods and goddesses are quite common throughout the country. Besides, the famous Shwe Dagon Pagoda of Yangon, whose foundation is supposed to be laid on the 'golden hairs' of the great *Buddha*, proclaims authoritatively the 2500 years of Indo-Burmese fellowship in culture and religion. The astrology in India had also left a permanent mark on the astronomy in Myanmar. The roots of Burmese Calendar are also imported from India (Soni 1955: 145).

There are also instances of marriage between the prince and princesses of India and Myanmar. In fact, the theme of a very popular play in Burma called 'Padeikkhaya' is the love of the Burmese princess of the Pagan days for an Indian prince beyond the seas (U Win 1948: 66). It has also been recorded that the valiant 'Arjuna' of the Mahabharata fame was having his honeymoon with Princess Chitragandha of Manipur amidst the picturesque landscape of Upper Burma (Soni 1955: 154-55).

The developments in India in the first six centuries of the Christian era had their due repercussions in Myanmar through the agency of visiting scholars and zealous missionaries. Besides, the cultural treasure of Aryans, Myanmar also considerably imbibed the spirit of the Pallava culture from the Deccan India. These influences largely contributed towards its cultural splendour, which is reflected amongst an estimated two million Hindus (which includes people from Bihar and UP, Marwaris, Gujratis, Bengalis, Tamils, Telgus and Nepalese) and four million Muslims in Myanmar (mostly migrated from Surat, Sindh and Pakistan).

The magnitude of Indian influence in Myanmar is so great that in order to have a proper grasp of the cultural trends in Burmese history, it is important to study the cultural evolutions in ancient India. In the words of Buddhist historian R.L. Soni, "There is certainly scope for further investigation and research….." this could make the Indo-Myanmar ties much stronger. The traditional relation of friendship and cooperation between the two countries could be deepened and intensified further to their mutual benefit. Since both the countries share a common thread of cultural ancestry, Myanmar has to learn a lot in modern times from Indian experience on the path of democratic development, which it has chosen since independence.

The Realist Paradigm

Cultural and historical ties gave way to close cooperation between India and Myanmar in their anti-colonial struggles. This, in turn, laid the strong foundation for the warm relationship between the two countries up to the early 1960s. "Burma's policy towards India in the post-independence decade was primarily guided by the zeal to control Indian immigration; to seek help from India for the reconstruction of its war devastated economy and for suppressing the bitter civil war, which emerged in the first two years after independence. Besides, Burma also desired to cooperate with India on the question of international peace and support in the diplomatic sphere" (Singh 1979: 52).

This relationship between India and Myanmar during the time of U Nu and Jawaharlal Nehru could not continue for long. The situation changed with the coup in which U Nu was replaced by military government led by General Ne Win in 1962 (Bhaskar 200: 356-258; Aung and Myint 2001: 88-90; Egreteau 2003; Lall 2006: 430-31; Khosla 2007: 592; Bhattacharya 2007: 27). In the decades that followed, with Myanmar's military rulers disinterested in interacting with the world, and India preoccupied with its own problems, the two neighbours drifted apart. Yet India continued to enjoy the public goodwill in Myanmar. This close relationship with Myanmar's people warmed considerably in the wake of the 1988 mass protests against military rule, with India emerging as a staunch critic of the military's repression and the sanctuary it provided to democracy activists fleeing the country. The relations were further strained when the Indian government bestowed the Jawaharlal Nehru Award for International Understanding in 1993 to the Nobel laureate Aung San Suu Kyi. It resulted in ordinary people looking to India for support in their struggle for democracy. But that support ceased from the mid-1990s with India adopting a "pragmatic policy" towards Myanmar. It began engaging the Generals and diluting its ideological stand on return to democracy. This shift was prompted by security concerns, economic and energy interests and the need to check China's mounting influence in Myanmar. India's policy towards Myanmar has, however, stabilized over time and its preference for pragmatism has spanned governments led by parties of different hues (Singh 2012).

India's policy towards Myanmar in the last two decade has thus been primarily directed by 'realist' paradigm and geo-strategic factors rather that deep ideological commitment to democracy. Ever since mid-1990s, India has tried to normalize relations with Myanmar regardless of the kind of government in power there. To quote J.N. Dixit, "while India remains committed to democracy and related values, there was no reason for India to unilaterally assume responsibility of creating democracies in other countries. This had to be the choice and responsibility of the people of the country concerned, in this case the people of Myanmar" (Dixit 2000). Responding to a question at the Plenary Session of the IISS Shangri-La dialogue held on 3 June 2006 in Singapore, that if India can help promote democracy in neighbouring military-ruled Myanmar, the then Defence Minister Pranab Mukherjee said, India's 'basic principle is to live in peaceful co-existence and we do not believe in exporting ideologies. It is for the people of the country to decide what type of government they would like to have'. However, instead of 'exporting democracy' to Myanmar, India could follow a more practical option of supporting Myanmar in building up its democratic institutions. Since, ancient Buddhist laws in Myanmar are derived from the laws of *'Manu'*, its modern transition process can well learn a lot from its Indian counterpart.

This purposeful shift by India from an idealistic foreign policy to one that was firmly anchored in *real-politick* has been the driving force behind the improvement of relations between the two countries since the 1990s. The ongoing pace of democratic reforms in Myanmar, in recent times, may however speed up India's engagement with the new regime. Even Daw Aung San Suu Kyi appears to have overcome her sadness over India's stand with the democracy movement in Myanmar. To quote Ms. Suu Kyi, "Well I was saddened then, but I got over sadness a long time ago… Politics involves a lot of pragmatism and if India felt that it was more pragmatic for them to follow a certain line, then that's the line they would follow and that might not be what we've wished for. But I don't think we have the right to condemn India or any other country for following the line that they thought was best for them."[2]

India's Myanmar policy, according to Ambassador Rajiv Bhatia (2011) "has been facing criticism from the idealists' camp, which blames New Delhi for abandoning the cause of democracy. Realists on the other hand have argued that its pro-democracy stance had driven Myanmar into 'China's lap' (Bhatia 2010)." Therefore, our relations are bound to be affected by what the new Myanmar government does in future. Given the pragmatic considerations shaped by internal security, external exigencies and changed policy prescriptions of the South Block, the rationale behind India's policy towards Myanmar in the present times has been guided by the considerations of geo-strategic location; bilateral economic cooperation; security, peace and stability on the borders; development and economic prosperity in the North-east; energy security and the Chinese dynamics (Kanwal 2010: 134-149; Lall 2006: 424-46; Egreteau: 2003; Aung and Myint 2001: 87-113; Routray 2011: 299-321).

Geo-Strategic Concerns

Given the shift in the global focus from trans-Atlantic to Asia Pacific, Myanmar has acquired a strategic position for the countries of the region. It adjoins India's sensitive North-eastern states and portions of Bangladesh. It shares an equally significant border with China. Thus, the northern frontier of Myanmar constitutes a tri-junction with Bangladesh, China and the eastern frontiers of India. Myanmar also serves as India's gateway to ASEAN as it is the only ASEAN country, which has land and maritime borders with India. On the other hand, it also serves as a gateway for China's entry into the Bay of Bengal and the Indian Ocean. Myanmar's role in providing China a shorter access route to Indian Ocean and South Asia is going to be crucial in the strategic scene of South Asia (Cartwright 2009: 414). In addition, Myanmar is an important country on the rim of the Bay of Bengal region. Hence, India could become Myanmar's window to the West. It can be the interface for Myanmar's relationship with the rest of SAARC. These geo-political concerns have largely guided the relations between the two countries. However, in recent times, there have been certain fluctuations in the relevance accorded to Myanmar in the strategic calculus of New Delhi (Bhaskar 2000: 349).

The geographical location of the two countries has facilitated collaborations in multilateral cooperation at the sub-regional level—both being members of the Bay of Bengal Initiative for Multi-Sectoral Technical and Economic Cooperation (BIMSTEC), Bangladesh-China-India-Myanmar Forum for Regional Cooperation (BCIM) and Mekong Ganga Cooperation (MGC). Besides, India is a full dialogue partner of ASEAN and enjoys observer status in ASEAN Inter Parliamentary Union, whereas Myanmar has observer status in SAARC.[3] The North-eastern India is an essential factor in extending linkages with the South-east Asian countries via Myanmar. However, lack of connectivity is an important bottleneck in this regard. The rejuvenation of the BCIM Initiative, MGC and BIMSTEC with active participation from India's North-eastern states, may work out wonders for the region.

Myanmar in the region of South-east Asia has been strategic for both India and China. In the absence of significant Western presence, Myanmar provides unique vantage point to observe Sino-Indian interaction (Ting 2010: 15). India has been considered as a land of opportunity by the new reformist regime in Myanmar. It has been characterized as a benign force and a useful third party, given the suspicions that exist regarding the role of China and the reservations China has about the Western powers. As China's interest widens westwards and India's interest widens eastward, there is bound to be contradictions and competitions. It is, therefore, essential for India to ensure that Myanmar does not become part of an exclusive 'area of influence' of other powers in the region. In this emerging multipolar Asian order, India-Myanmar must look forward to amicable relations with all countries on an equal level. They need to work towards security architecture with focus on non-traditional security issues that require cross-national collaborations. This advocates for identification of convergences with no unilateral dominance in the region.

Bilateral Cooperation

In the backdrop of the end of Myanmar's isolation in the nineties and engagement with India, economic cooperation between the two countries has made significant progress and the bilateral trade has reached US$ 1.8 billion. The range of areas covered by Indian projects is remarkable and includes roads, railways, telecom, power, energy, hydrocarbons, remote sensing, agriculture, industry, IT and education. The two countries have also signed a number of economic cooperation and bilateral investment promotion agreements to facilitate their ventures in each other's country. As of July 2012, India's investment in Myanmar reached US$ 273.5 million, ranking 13th in the line-up of foreign investors.

Myanmar's oil and gas has attracted the largest foreign investment. Three Indian companies are involved in this sector—ONGC, Gas India Limited and Essar Oil Limited. India has also been involved in hydro-power projects in Myanmar. Exim Bank has signed a US$ 60 million Line of Credit with Myanmar Foreign Trade Bank. NHPC has also signed an MoU for joint ventures in the *Chindwin* River basin. India has been providing development aid worth several thousand dollars for establishing new factories under Myanmar Ministry of Industry. Funding some of the projects under technical and economic cooperation programme has been another feature of Indo-Burmese partnership. Defense cooperation has also been marked by regular exchanges of high-level visits and bilateral military exercises.

India has started building an Advanced Centre for Agricultural Research and Education (ACARE) in Myanmar capital Nay Pyi Taw to train agriculturists in the country. The centre is being built at the Yezin University of Agriculture. India would provide technical assistance, including laboratory equipment, and Indian experts would train post-graduate students of Myanmar. To help promote the development of agriculture, India has also extended US$ 10 million worth of farming equipment to Myanmar. The equipment includes 300 tractors, 150 threshers, 228 cultivators and 431 ploughs.

As a close and friendly neighbour, India remains committed to extend all possible assistance and support to the process of national reconciliation and further strengthening of democracy in Myanmar. Eyeing deeper ties with the people of Myanmar, India has extended a grant of US$ one million for development in the Rakhine state that recently saw decades-old tension between ethnic Buddhist Rakhines and Muslim Rakhines. India and Myanmar also signed two MoUs for building a Rhi-Tiddim Road connecting the two countries and for setting up of a new Consulate in Sittwe, the capital of Rakhine State.

MAJOR INDIAN PROJECTS IN MYANMAR

The Government of India is actively involved in over a dozen projects in Myanmar, both in infrastructural and non-infrastructural areas. These include:

- Upgradation and resurfacing of the 160 km long Tamu-Kalewa-Kalemyo road;
- Construction and upgradation of the Rhi-Tiddim Road in Myanmar;
- The Kaladan Multimodal Transport Project;
- ADSL project for high-speed data link in 32 Myanmar cities has been completed by TCIL.
- ONGC Videsh Ltd. (OVL), GAIL and ESSAR are participants in the energy sector in Myanmar.
- M/s RITES is involved in the development of the rail transportation system and in the supply of railway coaches, locos and parts.
- In September 2008, Ministry of Electric Power-1 (MoEP-1) and NHPC signed an agreement for the development of the Tamanthi and Shwezaye Hydro-Electric Power project in Chindwin River valley.
- A heavy turbo-truck assembly plant set up in Myanmar by TATA Motors with GOI financial assistance was inaugurated on December 31, 2010.
- An India-Myanmar Industrial Training Centre has been set up by HMT(I) in Myanmar with the assistance of GOI in Pakokku, a second centre is being set up in Myingyan.
- Myanmar-India Centre for English Language (MICELT);
- Myanmar-India Entrepreneurship Development Centre (MIEDC) and;
- India-Myanmar Centre for Enhancement of IT Skills (IMCEITS);
- Restoration of the Ananda Temple in Bagan;
- Upgradation of the Yangon Children's Hospital and Sittwe General Hospital;
- Erection of disaster proof rice silos; and
- In the reconstruction of one high school and six primary schools in Tarlay township, the area worst affected by the severe earthquake that struck north-eastern Myanmar in March 2011.

(*Source*: India-Myanmar relation, July 2012. http:// www.mea.gov.in/.../india-myanmar-relations-24-05-2012-press-release.pdf).

Security, Peace and Stability on the Borders

India's perception of security and stability in the Northeast has been influenced by the use of Myanmar as a base by Indian insurgents. The porous border of the Northeast India with Myanmar has been a flourishing ground for drug trafficking and illegal arms trade in the region. Several incidents of insurgency, together with the ethnic conflicts in the border areas have created troubles for both countries. India has sought cooperation from Myanmar in its counter insurgency operations in the northeastern states along Myanmar border and held several joint military operations. India and Myanmar have showed commitment to strengthen bilateral cooperation to eliminate nexus between the drug trade, arms smuggling, extremism and insurgency for establishing peace and security in the region.

Drug Trafficking

Northeast India shares a long and porous border with Myanmar, and cross border smuggling of narcotics has been one of the main sources of income for most insurgent groups in the region. It has been reported that Myanmar is the second largest opium growing country after Afghanistan and the largest producer of methamphetamines (ATS-type drugs) (Egrteau 2006: 133). Ethnic conflict as well as the underground economic interests of insurgent outfits on both sides of the Indo-Burmese border has widely facilitated the sale and smuggling of drugs on a large scale (*ibid*)[4]. Chemicals used in the preparation of heroin and methamphetamines are said to be imported from India, and finished heroin is exported to India, some of which has been confiscated by the Indian authorities. Intravenous drug use has led to 70 per cent HIV rate among users in the region (Steinberg 2009; Egrteau 2003). Increase in the arms and drug trafficking and cross border support has undermined India's relations with Myanmar and requires India to be more actively involved in the region. According to a report, inefficient handling of the border areas and collusion between the regional authorities of the two countries are the primary reason for the flourishing of the regional drug trafficking network (Mizzima News 2004).

Arms Smuggling

Illicit smuggling of arms and ammunition across India's North-eastern states bordering Myanmar has added to the growing concern for peace and security in the region. North-eastern India has been wrecked by insurgency since 1950s with various groups flourishing as a result of illegal arms trade from across the borders. These groups with the support of arms have posed a threat to the unity and integrity of both countries. As cited by Gurmeet Kanwal (2010 b), "Chinese weapons gained immense popularity among the insurgent groups in the region, as they were competitively priced and offered with countertrade agreements." The problem gets compounded also due to the fact that there is a free movement regime between India and Myanmar that facilitates the cross-border smuggling of small arms.

Extremism and Insurgency

India shares more than 1600 km long border with Myanmar with three check points, but the incidence of illegal migrants has increased over the years.[5] Up to 100,000 Christian Chin have fled to India in the past 20 years to escape persecution by Myanmar's Buddhist military rulers. The north-east region in India has been witnessing rising violence through ethnic and criminal clashes. Myanmar has served as a corridor linking the north-eastern insurgent groups and many of them have established bases in Myanmar (Egrteau 2003). The border of India and Myanmar has been porous and the Indian insurgents in the north-eastern states are seeking refuge in deep jungles (Cartwright 2009: 414).

Since independence, ethnic minorities in both countries are struggling against their respective governments for autonomy and their political and cultural recognition (Egrteau 2003: 7). In India, the Naga rebels, United Liberation Front from Assam (ULFA), Mizo National Front in Mizoram and several other resurgent groups have been involved in ethnic and violent clashes and north-east India has become the den of illicit drugs and weapons trafficking. Many of these groups have taken shelter beyond the Indo-Burmese border. Some of the insurgent groups like the National Socialist Council of

Nagaland (NSCN) and the ULFA operate from sanctuaries in Myanmar (Egrteau 2006: 133; Hariharan 2007). These insurgents, together with the Burmese rebellions on its side of the border have created troubles for both countries (Steinberg 2009).

In order to curb illegal migration, on 21 January 1994, a Memorandum of Understanding (MoU) was signed to increase cooperation between the civilian border authorities of the two countries to prevent "illegal and insurgent activities". A further bilateral agreement was signed to regularize and promote border trade, which officially resumed on 12 April 1995; and a cross-border post between Moreh (Manipur, India) and Tamu (Sagaing Division, Myanmar) was opened (Egreteau 2006: 138). This agreement enhanced the bilateral border trade between the two countries. Furthermore, at the military level in 1995, both armies decided to conduct a first joint military operation (called *Operation Golden Bird*) against some insurgent groups in North-east India. This was aimed at dismantling ULFA, NSCN and other insurgent camps. This joint operation was successful in considerably weakening the militant outfits by killing or arresting many of their cadres (*ibid*). In July 2010, Major General Than Shwe and Prime Minister Manmohan Singh agreed upon a strategy to increase security cooperation and strengthen collective efforts to fight the insurgents and combat terrorism along the border of the two countries. It was decided that India and Myanmar will conduct a 'coordinated operation' against Indian north-east separatist outfits taking shelter and setting up base camps in the neighbouring country (Assam Tribune 2010).

India has sought Myanmar's cooperation for coordinated patrolling along the border and dismantling camps of Indian insurgent groups (IIGs) in its territory. Both sides expressed satisfaction over opening of a third Border Liaison Office (BLO) between Changlang and Pangsau and decided to open the fourth BLO in the Nagaland sector between Ukhrul in Manipur and Somra in Myanmar (Press Information Bureau, 2013). Both sides agreed to cooperate closely on curbing of insurgent activities along the border, on issues of arms smuggling, drug trafficking, border management and the presence of Myanmar fishermen in Andaman and Nicobar jails.

Development and Economic Prosperity in the North-east India

Development and economic prosperity in the north-eastern part of India has been a guiding principle behind India's Myanmar policy (Aung and Myint 2001: 98; Egreteau 2003; 2006; Lall 2006: 422). The lack of economic opportunities in the region combined with high level of insurgency and extremist activities with cross-border linkages have raised concerns for the overall stability and development of the region (Bhaskar 2000: 358). In this regard, the proximity of the North-eastern region with Myanmar offers immense opportunities. It has the potential of strengthening closer political ties between the two countries.

Infrastructure development and rail-road connectivity beginning from north-eastern India running through Myanmar will serve as India's 'Gateway to South-east Asia' and beyond. It will also act as a major trade route for linking the landlocked region of north-east to the ports of South-east Asia. Efforts have been made in this direction through Kaladan Multi-Modal Transit Transport Project to enhance the connectivity between the two countries, especially with the north-eastern states (Indian Express 2008). This is supposed to provide an important access point for linking not only India's hitherto landlocked north-east, but also a viable trade route from the countries of South-east Asia, such as Indonesia, Malaysia and Singapore. The project envisages linking Kolkata seaport with Siitwe port in Myanmar, further linking Sittwe to Mizoram via river and road transport. It hopes to improve the connectivity between Indian ports on the eastern seaboard and Sittwe Port in Myanmar and then through riverine transport and by road to Mizoram, thereby providing an alternate route for transport of goods to north-east India. The project also seeks to provide connectivity between India and Myanmar, which will lead to the development of trade between the two countries. It will also contribute to economic development of Mizoram and other North-eastern states[6].

Besides, reviving old rail-road links from Assam to Vietnam is also high on the Indian agenda. A trilateral highway linking India, Myanmar and Thailand to improve connectivity, increase trade and develop the regions economically has also been taken up on priority basis. This is going to boost trade and investment not only in the three countries, but also the four states of north-east India that share borders with Myanmar. Furthermore, renovation and re-opening of the historic Stilwell Road is significant as it could make the North-east region a gateway for India's trade along the corridor through Myanmar, running into Kunming in China.

Special mention may be made here with regard to the India-ASEAN Car Rally[7] and the recently started BCIM car rally.[8] Both car rallies are an attempt to restore the transport connectivity and revive the ancient trade route, and Myanmar is the common link. BCIM car rally seeks to revive commercial trade in the 'Southern Silk Route' with a 3,000-km car rally from Kolkata to Kunming in China via Myanmar (Indian Express 2013). Identifying the common need for regional connectivity and building a development corridor with the focus on the development of North-east India through increased trade and commerce is the idea behind having these car rallies.

The development of the existing border trade points with Myanmar and exploring the new ones also requires immediate attention. As of now, there are two operational border trade points, Moreh-Tamu and Zowkhatar-Rhi along the 1643 km border. A third border trade point is proposed to be opened at Avakhung-Pansat/ Somrai.[9]

Energy Security

Energy is important not only for economic growth and prosperity, but also for social progress and stability. It forms the most important element of national security in most of the countries and 'energy politics' has become increasingly important for the Asian region (Lall 2006: 426-27; Fengying and Jiejun 2008: 52). Myanmar's oil and gas reserves are of critical interest to India's future energy requirement (Routray 2011). Both India and China have been witnessing fierce competition and rivalry owing to the increased consumption of energy, which has been a result of increased economic growth characterized by high industrial activity. The quest for energy security has resulted in exploring hydrocarbon reserves and gas options in Myanmar (Datta 2008: 104). Natural gas has become one of Myanmar's key export commodities.

After the discovery of huge natural gas deposits off the Rakhine coast in 2003, India started exploring options for meeting its energy requirements through gas fields in Shwe, located in the northern most point of the Rakhine offshore area. It was felt that the energy needs of eastern India and most particularly, the north-eastern states could be well served by Myanmar's gas compared to other sources. By offering attractive investments in Myanmar's energy sector, India sought to further strengthen its ties with Myanmar in the face of parallel Chinese interest in Myanmar's gas; and its increasing political, economic and military activities in Myanmar including its increased naval presence in the Bay of Bengal and in the Straits of Malacca. The proposed pipeline route was to pass through Bangladesh resulting in a tripartite pipeline arrangement among India-Bangladesh-Myanmar. This could have helped in balancing the Chinese influence in the region. But given the reluctance of Bangladesh and finally its refusal to become a party to the tripartite agreement, Indo-Myanmar gas pipeline became untenable.

This lost opportunity was a gain for China. China has been able to diversify the routes of its energy imports by building a pipeline running from Myanmar's coasts along the Indian Ocean to Yunnan directly (Ting 2010: 19). An agreement was signed with Petro-China where Myanmar agreed to sell oil through an overland pipeline to Kunming in China for 30 years. China is also involved in Shwe Gas project off Myanmar's Western coast (Embassy of India: Yangoon). Myanmar's decision to tie up with the Chinese firm Petro-China was a setback for Indian oil diplomacy and its energy security (Hariharan 2007).

Nevertheless, India's GAIL and ONGC have entered into Oil Block Agreements for offshore operation in A1 and A3 gas blocks in the Shwe Gas Project.[10] Essar has been operating in the Rakhine offshore A2 block and Sittwe onshore PSC-L block (Ministry of Energy, Myanmar). State-owned GAIL (India) Ltd. plans to pick up 4.17 per cent equity in the US$ 2.01 billion pipeline for exporting gas from Myanmar to southern China in the proposed Myanmar-China Gas Pipeline Project. ONGC Videsh (OVL), the overseas investment arm of state-owned Oil and Natural Gas Corporation (ONGC), has also plans to buy 8.35 per cent equity in the Myanmar-China gas pipeline project (DNA 2010). Recently, Myanmar has invited foreign energy companies to bid for the right to explore 18 onshore oil and gas blocks (Myanmar Times 2013).

Chinese Dynamics

India-Myanmar relations are also guided by the threat perception that Chinese influence in Myanmar poses to India's interest in the region. The reluctance in maintaining friendly relations by India during military crackdown in the late 1980s and support for the pro-democratic activities was to the Chinese advantage as they made inroads in Myanmar around the same time. "China has majorly expanded in Myanmar and this has facilitated China's entry into the Bay of Bengal. India needs to have a countervailing presence in Myanmar to ensure that its own interests are not jeopardized" (Saran 2011).

There had been an enormous growth in China's influence in Myanmar, significantly, after the western nations imposed sanctions on Myanmar since 1989 in the wake of pro-democratic protests and its violent crackdown (Lee *et al.* 2009: 102). Besides, as Burmese junta opened and liberalized the economy in the early 1990s, China became a natural ally. The armed forces of Myanmar depend largely on Chinese assistance. Furthermore, the support of China has been crucial in diplomatic fora, such as the United Nations Security Council. Increasing Chinese access to Myanmar's energy resources is a matter of concern for India because of its strategic implications. Due to growing Sino-Myanmar energy ties, China is investing heavily in developing ports in Myanmar, gaining greater access to the Indian Ocean. In the wake of sanctions, Western investments in Myanmar was blocked for long, providing opportunity to China to emerge as Myanmar's biggest ally, investing in infrastructure, hydropower dams and twin oil-and-gas pipelines, which has helped feed China's growing energy needs.

Myanmar also occupies a critical space on China's south-western flank. Economically, Myanmar is important for China as a trading outlet to the Indian Ocean for its landlocked inland provinces of Yunnan and Sichuan. China's Myanmar policy has been dictated to a large extent by what will help Yunnan's economy move forward. According to Thant Myint (2011), "For much of its early history, Burma's neighbour to the north-east was not China, but the independent Kingdom of Yunnan". Yunnanese companies are big investors in mining, rubber and other industries in the bordering state of Kachin in Myanmar. Therefore, officials in Yunnan have a keen interest in keeping the ethnic clashes in Border States calm. The Burmese market was seen as a major opportunity for cheap Chinese products. Ever since then, Myanmar has been largely dominated by Chinese investors and traders gathering timber, jade and rubber (Egrteau 2003: 12). Yunnan needs to be compared with India's neglected north-eastern States.

The Chinese strategists also see Myanmar as the bridge to the Bay of Bengal and the waters beyond. This was a matter of serious concern for India as it brought the threat from Chinese mainland nearer home to the northeast. There are two other factors influencing China's calculations. China sees Myanmar as having an increasingly important role in its energy security. Another factor impacting Beijing's strategy towards Myanmar is the US Administration's engagement policy. There is an apprehension that a democratic Myanmar will become a pro-US Myanmar. With the United States entering Myanmar's diplomatic scene, China has appointed a special envoy to focus on Nay Pyi Taw's dealings with the world (Times of India 2013).

Despite the recent setbacks to Chinese investments in Myanmar,[11] Beijing's economic presence in the country continues to grow with the oil and gas pipeline almost ready to transport oil as an alternative route from Africa and Persian Gulf by the end of 2013. It also plans to build a highway and a high speed railway line by 2015, which would allow people and cargo to travel from Kyaukpyu passing through Mandalay to Yunnan. This would later be connected to Chittagong in Bangladesh, thus joining up Yunnan to Bangladesh via Myanmar through a Tri-nation highway. Chinese companies are also developing large SEZs and power plants and devising strategies for building a deep water commercial seaport at Kyaukpyu's natural harbour (Raja Mohan 2013). This would satisfy China's urge for energy security as well as link to Bay of Bengal and the Indian Ocean.

Strengthening Partnership

Re-engagement with the new regime through high-level visits has been a regular feature of India-Myanmar relations for several years. After the formation of the new government led by President U Thein Sein on 30 March, 2011, Shri S.M. Krishna, the Minister of External Affairs, was the first high-level dignitary to visit Myanmar on 20-22 June, 2011. President U Thein Sein paid a State visit to India on 12-15 October, 2011. The visit represented the first State visit from Myanmar to India following the swearing-in of a new Government in Myanmar in March 2011. India and Myanmar agreed to a series of measures to boost trade and co-operation during the visit. *Pyithu Hluttaw* (Lower House) Speaker Thura U Shwe Mann led a high-level parliamentary delegation to India from 11 to 17 December, 2011. The objective of the visit was to share India's experience in parliamentary practices and procedures with the visiting Myanmar delegation. Myanmar Foreign Minister U Wunna Maung Lwin paid an official visit to India from 22 to 26 January, 2012. This was followed by the Prime Minister Manmohan Singh's visit from 28 to 30 May 2012. Prime Minister Manmohan Singh's visit was historic, as it was the first official visit to Myanmar by an Indian Prime Minister since 1987. On this occasion, the two sides signed 12 agreements to strengthen trade and diplomatic ties. Daw Aung San Suu Kyi visited India from 13 to 16 November 2012 to deliver Jawaharlal Nehru Memorial lecture. External Affairs Minister Mr. Salman Khurshid made his first official visit to the country from 14 to 16 December 2012, where he met the President, his counterpart, Foreign Affairs Minister Wunna Maung Lwin, and top officials. He inaugurated a three-day international conference on 'Buddhist Cultural Heritage' attended by scholars from ten countries, apart from monks and teachers. This was followed by unveiling of a 15-foot replica of the statue of Gautam Buddha in the precincts of the Shwedagon Pagoda, which was gifted by Prime Minister Manmohan Singh during his visit to Myanmar in May 2012.

President Thein Sein paid second visit to India during ASEAN-India Commemorative Summit on 20 December 2012. Defence Minister A.K. Antony led a delegation to Myanmar from 21 to 22 January 2013. Both sides discussed modalities for improving mechanisms for patrolling by their own forces along with the land and maritime boundaries to curb activities of insurgent groups and other illegal and criminal activities in these areas. Both sides agreed that neither side should allow their territory to be used for activities detrimental to the security of the other. Both countries agreed to conduct periodic coordinated land and maritime patrols. Smt. Meira Kumar, Speaker of Lok Sabha visited Myanmar with a Parliamentary delegation from 12 to 15 February, 2013. These series of high-level delegation in just a period of two years is a symbol of considerable political and strategic significance both countries attach to each other in the changed political landscape of Myanmar after transition.

The visit by Indian Speaker is an example of cooperation in cultivating and evolving a culture of democratic practice in Myanmar. Besides, Bureau of Parliamentary Studies and Training (BPST) of the Lok Sabha Secretariat have provided support in capacity-building of Myanmar's MPs and parliamentary officials. Two programmes for 30 Members of Myanmar Parliament were organized at BPST in July and October 2012, which enabled them to interact with senior Indian parliamentarians on issues, such as legislative processes, budgetary processes, parliamentary questions and other procedural devices to raise matters on the floor of the House, committee system, parliamentary privileges, support services for MPs, etc. Similarly, another set of 30 middle level officers of the Myanmar Parliament attended two separate programmes in the BPST in June and September 2012. Furthermore, at the invitation of the Government of Myanmar, India sent senior officials from the Election Commission and journalists from the official media as observers for the by-elections in April 2012.

In the wake of the regime transformation and emerging dynamics in Myanmar with the emergence of the western powers and rapprochement with the United States, India will now have to push more vigorously to expand its economic interests in Myanmar before the West starts making its presence felt. India's economic involvement in Myanmar, largely through the public sector, has not been up to the mark with complaints about implementation delays and quality controls. This gap, however, must be filled by the Indian private sector; those who want to move to Myanmar as opportunities expand in the country. Building of rail-road connectivity through Myanmar to Southeast Asia and reviving old rail-road links from Assam to Vietnam demands immediate attention. Investment in agriculture, industry, banking sector, education, health, transport and communication is urgently required by India, besides its existing share in pearls and pulses, timber, oil and natural gas projects. Last, but not the least, Track II diplomacy at the level of civil society, cultural and academic exchanges will go a long way in strengthening people-to-people contact between the two countries. Business conclaves, delegations and trade fairs may also give boost to developing business-to-business contacts and strengthening bilateral relations between the two countries.

The Challenges

Given the political transformation in Myanmar, the country offers immense opportunities for re-engagement, which India may use for its strategic advantage. However, it is not free from caveat. The road ahead is full of challenges.

India has now a greater responsibility being the world's largest democracy and one of Myanmar's closest neighbours having civilizational ties. It has to keep up to the rising expectations of the pro-democratic forces in Myanmar. Even the opposition leader, Daw Aung San Suu Kyi could not hide her emotions when she advocated a greater role for India in Myanmar. To quote her, "Myanmar had not yet achieved the goal of democracy... We hope that through this difficult last stage, the people of India will stand by us and walk with us as we proceed along the path, which they had taken many years before."[12]

Easing of western sanctions after political reforms in Myanmar has compelled India to take a more proactive role. It has to secure its own economic interest vis-à-vis the competition against the new powers in the region. As of now, European Union and Australia have lifted their travel and financial sanctions against Myanmar, but the United States has taken what U.S. officials call a "calibrated" approach. While it has suspended most restrictions on investment, imports and financial services, the U.S. still maintains its list of targeted sanctions, bans some people from travelling to the U.S. and blocks imports of specific products, such as jade and rubies, for which trade has been dominated by state and military interests.

In the current phase of transformation, the Chinese support for the regime seems to be a challenging opportunity, particularly, vis-à-vis its growing rapprochement with the West and its closeness with India. Myanmar seems to be walking on a tight rope in balancing both China and India together. It is certain to give precedence to democratic administrative practices of state building and nation building as against the previous regimes. This has brought Myanmar closer to India than its earlier Big Brother, China. It poses a considerable threat to the long Chinese influence and dominance in the region. The threat has become more real after the suspension of the US$ 3.6 billion Myitsone dam project and recent protest against a China-backed copper mine in north-western Myanmar at Letpadaung near Monywa. Nevertheless, China continues to remain as its second-largest trading partner (Thailand ranks at the top while India stands at fourth) and biggest source of foreign investments. On the other hand, President Thein Sein in his September 2012 visit to China has reaffirmed that Myanmar's transition to democracy will not change the country's traditional friendship with China. The two countries have agreed to continue to strengthen communication and coordination to accelerate the formulation of mid-term and long-term goals of bilateral exchanges in politics, economy, trade, culture, security and other areas to steadily push forward comprehensive cooperation.

Indian public sector investment in Myanmar has not been enough and it is marred by bureaucratic hurdles and procedural delays. This needs an introspection and greater intervention by the private players. In the absence of a democratic culture in Myanmar, it is very difficult to carry out negotiations and implement democratic administrative practices. Furthermore, lack of connectivity and poor rail-road link in the border areas of Myanmar and India's north-eastern region has posed a formidable challenge in integrating the region and reaping the benefits of development dividends. In this regard, the budget speech of the finance minister P. Chidambaram has been a welcome move, which has focused on building up of road connectivity between the north-east and Myanmar under India's Look East policy. This would be developed with the assistance of the World Bank and the Asian Development Bank.[13]

The ultimate determining point would be the internal political dynamics within the political regime and its long-term repercussions on the India-Myanmar relations. The ongoing tussle between the hardliners and the reformist has slowed down the reform process. This poses a question over the durability and sustainability of the regime. However, it is considered that a stable Myanmar would be to the advantage of India. In addition, the relationship between Daw Aung San Suu Kyi and the military and the dynamics, which she shares with other opposition parties will determine the structure of the regime and its consequence on India-Myanmar relations. Resolving the ethnic issue will be Myanmar's biggest challenge now. It needs to learn lessons from India in the field of federal democratic practices and managing ethnic conflicts.

Regime transformation and political developments in Myanmar since the last two years have opened new chapter in India-Myanmar relations. This could pave the way for strengthening partnership in the years to come. Despite having close ties in the initial years after independence during the period of parliamentary democracy and the subsequent strains during the military rule to its present policy shift from 'idealism to realism' and engagement with Myanmar, the two countries have continued to remain as 'good brothers'. Change in the regime structure has been a guiding factor in oscillating bilateral relationship. However, people-to-people contact has continued between the two countries in the form of cultural and spiritual exchanges. In this regard, Daw Aung Suu Kyi stated "I always had faith in the lasting friendship of India and Myanmar, which was based on love and kinship between the people of the two countries....This is what I wish to emphasize again and again. Friendship between countries should be based on friendship between people and not friendship between governments... Governments come and go and that is what democracy is all about. But, people remain, and as long as the two countries' people have good understanding and mutual respect, the friendship between the two countries will last far into the future[14]."

NOTES

1. Based on Daw Aung San Suu Kyi's Jawaharlal Nehru Memorial Lecture, November 14, 2012.
2. Based on Daw Aung San Suu Kyi's interview to NDTV November 15, 2012. http://www.ndtv.com/article/india/full-transcript-my-farewell-message-for-my-husband-was-too-late-says-aung-san-suu-kyi-to-ndtv-292831.
3. India became a sectoral dialogue partner of ASEAN in 1992, which was upgraded to full dialogue partnership in 1996. Since 2002, India has had annual Summits with ASEAN. India's approval for observer status at the ASEAN Inter-Parliamentary Assembly (AIPA) was approved in 2010. Myanmar was given the status of observer in SAARC in August 2008.
4. Manipur and Nagaland borders serve as an easy access for the smuggling of opium. It is easily refined into heroin in factories run by local drug lords in the regions surrounding Moreh and Imphal. The entire border region and National Highway has become a lawless area run by ultras and traffickers and are very difficult to cross (Egreteau 2006: 134).
5. Based on the report of the Ministry of Overseas Indian Affairs. Available: http://www.moia.gov.in/pdf/Myanmar.pdf
6. Ministry of Development of Northeast Region, Government of India. http://www.mdoner.gov.in/content/introduction-1.
7. The 1st ASEAN-India Car Rally was held from 23 November-6 December 2004, which involved about 240 participants with 60 vehicles. Then, the journey started in Guwahati, India, and traversed to Myanmar, Thailand, the Lao PDR, Viet Nam, Cambodia, Malaysia and Singapore before ending in Batam, Indonesia covering a total distance of 8,000 km. The 2nd edition of the

ASEAN-India Car Rally that involved over 120 participants from ASEAN Member States and India and included more than 30 cars. The Rally started on 26 November 2012 in Yogyakarta, Indonesia, and concluded in New Delhi on 20 December 2012.

8. The Bangladesh-China-India-Myanmar Forum for Regional Cooperation (BCIM) hopes to retrace the lost trails and revive commercial trade in the 'Southern Silk Route' with a 3,000-km car rally from Kolkata to Kunming in China.
9. Based on ASEAN-India Report on India-Myanmar relation, July 2012. http://www.aseanindia.com/wp-content/uploads/2012/10/myanmar-july-2012.pdf
10. Oil and Natural Gas Corp (ONGC) had 20 per cent stake and GAIL 10 per cent stake in A-1 and A-3 offshore blocks.
11. The suspension of the US$3.6 billion dam project at Myitsone, the biggest of seven planned by China Power Investment in Myanmar has left the leadership in China stunned. The recent protest against a China-backed copper mine in northwestern Myanmar has added to the Chinese apprehensions. These have raised alarm bells for leadership in Beijing.
12. Based on impromptu remarks at the end of Aung San Suu Kyi's speech at the Jawaharlal Nehru Memorial Lecture 14 November 2012. http://www.indianexpress.com/news/india-was-aloof-in-our-hard-days-suu-kyi/1031266/0.
13. Based on the Budget Speech 2013 of Finance Minister P. Chidambaram.
14. Based on impromptu remarks at the end of Aung San Suu Kyi's speech at the Jawaharlal Nehru Memorial Lecture 14 November 2012. http://www.indianexpress.com/news/india-was-aloof-in-our-hard-days-suu-kyi/1031266/0.

REFERENCES

ASEAN-India Report on India-Myanmar relation, July 2012. Accessed on February 18, 2013. URL: http://www.aseanindia.com/wp-content/uploads/2012/10/myanmar-july-2012.pdf

Assam Tribune (2010), "India Myanmar to jointly fight Northeast rebels", February 28. Accessed on March 18, 2013. URL: http://www.assamtribune.com/scripts/detailsnew.asp?id=feb2810/at044

Aung San Suu Kyi (2012), "Discovery of Nehru", Jawaharlal Nehru Memorial Lecture, November 14, 2012. Full text of the speech accessed on January 19, 2013. URL: http://www.hindustantimes.com/India-news/NewDelhi/Full-text-of-Suu-Kyi-s-Jawaharlal-Nehru-Memorial-Lecture/Article1-959856.aspx

Aung, Thin Thin and Soe Myint, 2001. *India-Burma Relations*, pp. 87-113. Accessed on March 13, 2013. URL: http://www.idea.int/asia_pacific/burma/upload/challenges_to_democratization_in_burma.pdf

Bhaskar, C. Uday (2000), 'Myanmar in the Strategic Calculus of India and China,' in *The Peacock and the Dragon: India-China Relations in the 21st Century*, ed. Kanti Bajpai and Amitabh Mattoo, New Delhi: Har-Anand Publications.

Bhatia, Rajiv (2010), "Crafting a richer India-Myanmar partnership", *The Hindu*, Wednesday, August 11.

Bhatia, Rajiv (2011), "Myanmar: Challenges and Way Forward", *The Hindu*, July 4.

Bhattacharya, Swapna (2007), *India Myanmar Relation: 1886-1948*, Kolkatta: K.P. Bagchi & Company.

Budget Speech 2013 of Finance Minister P. Chidambaram. Accessed on March 2, 2013. URL: http://indiabudget.nic.in/bspeecha.asp

Cartwright, J (2009), India's Regional and International Support for Democracy: Rhetoric or Reality? *Asian Survey,* Volume 49(3), pp. 403-428.

Chakravarti, Nalini Ranjan (1971), *Indian Minority in Myanmar*, Oxford University Press: London.

Datta, Sreeradha (2008), "Bangladesh factor in the Indo Myanmarese Gas Deal", *Strategic Analysis*, Vol. 32(1), pp. 103-122.

DNA (2010), "GAIL, ONGC Videsh buying Myanmar pipeline stake", January 19. Accessed on March 19, 2013. URL: http://www.dnaindia.com/money/report_gail-ongc-videsh-buying-myanmar-pipeline-stake_1336407

Dixit, J.N. (2000), "India and Myanmar in a crucial relationship", *India News*, Online Edition, Accessed on February 1, 2013, URL: http://news.indiamart.com/index.html

Egreteau, Renaud (2003), "India-Myanmar Relations: From Idealism to Realism", Paper presented at a Conference, India International Centre, New Delhi.

Egreteau, Renaud (2006), Instability at the Gate: India's Troubled Northeast and its External Connections, CSH, Occasional Paper No. 16.

Embassy of India, Yangoon, India-Myanmar Commercial Relations. URL: http://www.indiaembassy.net.mm/commercial/commercial_relations_3.asp. Accessed on April 8, 2010.

Fengying, Chen and Jiejun Ni (2008), "Asian Energy Security: The Role of China and India", *Strategic Analysis*, Vol. 32(1), pp. 41-55

Hariharan R. (2007), "India-Myanmar-China Relations", *Asian Tribune*, Online Edition. Accessed on January 15, 2013, URL: http://www.asiantribune.com/categories/article

Harvey, G. E (1947), *Outline of Burmese History*, Orient Longman.

Indian Express (2008), "India, Myanmar ink Kaladan Multi-Modal Transit Transport Pact", 03 April.

Indian Express (2012), "India was aloof in our hard days", November 15. Online edition. Accessed on January 19, 2013. URL: http://www.indianexpress.com/news/india-was-aloof-in-our-hard-days-suu-kyi/1031266/0

Indian Express (2013), "BCIM Car Rally to Revive Southern Silk Route", February 21.

Kanwal, Gurmeet (2010), "A Strategic Perspective on India-Myanmar Relations", in Alexis Rieffel (ed) *Myanmar/Burma: Inside Challenges, Outside Interests,* Brookings Institution Press, pp. 134-149.

Kanwal, Gurmeet and Monika Chansoria (2010 b), "Small arms proliferation in South Asia" CLAWS, Issue Brief 18. Accessed on 28 March, 2013. URL: http://www.claws.in/administrator/uploaded_files/1274853671IB-18.pdf

Khosla, I.P. (2007), "India-Myanmar", in Atish Sinha and Madhup Mohta (eds), *Indian Foreign Policy: India's Foreign Policy: Challenges and Opportunities*, Academic Foundation: New Delhi, pp. 583-612.

Lal, Marie (2006), "Indo-Myanmar Relations in the era of pipeline diplomacy", *Contemporary Southeast Asia*, Vol. 28(3), pp. 424-46.

Lee Pak K., Gerald Chan & Lai-Ha Chan (2009), "China's *"Realpolitik* "Engagement with Myanmar" China *Security* Vol. 5(1), pp. 101-123.

Majumdar, R.C. (1955), *Ancient Indian Colonisation in Southeast Asia*, Baroda Oriental Institute. Quoted in Nalini Ranjan Chakravarti, *Indian Minority in Myanmar*, Oxford University Press, 1971.

MEA (2012), *India-Myanmar Relations*, Accessed on February 15, 2013. URL: http://www.mea.gov.in/Images/pdf/india-myanmar-relations-24-05-2012-press-release.pdf

Ministry of Development of Northeast Region, Government of India. Kaladan Multi-Modal Transit Transport Project. Accessed on March 15, 2013. URL: http://www.mdoner.gov.in/content/introduction-1

Ministry of Energy, Myanmar. Accessed on March 25. URL: http://www.energy.gov.mm/index.php/en/about-moe/menu-moge

Ministry of Overseas Indian Affairs, Myanmar. Accessed on January 12, 2013. URL: http://www.moia.gov.in/pdf/Myanmar.pdf

Mizzima News Report (2004), India-Burma - Drug Cultivation, Consumption and Trafficking. URL: http://www.mizzima.com/component/content/article/1559.html

Myanmar Times (2013), "Plans announced for offshore, onshore bids at Myanmar oil and gas summit", Accessed on March 19, 2013. URL: http://www.mmtimes.com/index.php/business/4332-plans-announced-for-offshore-onshore-bids-at-myanmar-oil-and-gas-summit.html

NDTV (2012), Full Transcript, Daw Aung San Suu Kyi's interview to NDTV November 15, 2012.Accessed on January 19, 2013. URL: http://

www.ndtv.com/article/india/full-transcript-my-farewell-message-for-my-husband-was-too-late-says-aung-san-suu-kyi-to-ndtv-292831

Press Information Bureau, Govt. of India (2013), "18th National Level Meeting between Myanmar and India", Press Release, January 3. Accessed on March 21, 2013. URL: http://pib.nic.in/newsite/erelease.aspx?relid=91320

Raja Mohan, C (2013), "Bengal's Waters", *Indian Express*, March 13.

Routray, B.P. (2011), "India-Myanmar Relations: Triumph of Prgamatism", *Jindal Journal of International Affairs*, pp. 299-321

Soni, R.L. (1955), *The Cultural Study of Burmese Era*, Institute of Buddhist Culture, Mandalay.

Saran, Shyam (2011), "India's strategic interest in Myanmar", IPCS Special Report 98, Accessed on February 20. URL: http://www.ipcs.org/pdf_file/issue/SR98-ShyamSaranInterview.pdf

Singh, Udai Bhanu (2012), "An Assessment of Manmohan Singh's visit to Myanmar", IDSA Issue Brief. Accessed on February 3, 2013. URL: http://idsa.in/issuebrief/AnAssessmentofManmohanSinghsVisittoMyanmar

Singh, Uma Shankar (1979), *Burma and India: 1948-1962*, Oxford and IBH Publishing Company.

Steinberg, David (2009), "Prospects for Democratisation in Myanmar: Impact on India", *Indian Defense Review*, Vol. 24(4). Accessed on January 24, 2013.Online edition. URL: http://www.ndiandefencereview.com/category/vol-244-oct-dec-2009.

Suryanarayan, V. (2009), The Indian Community in Myanmar, *SAAG*, Paper No. 3523. Online article. URL: http://www.southasiaanalysis.org/%5Cpapers36%5Cpaper3523.html

Suu Kyi, Aung San (1990), *Burma and India: Some Aspects of Intellectual Life under Colonialism,* Shimla, New Delhi: Indian Institute of Advanced Studies& Allied Publishers.

Thant, Myint U (2011), *Where China Meets India: Burma and the New Crossroads of Asia*, Faber and Faber Limited London.

Ting, M.H. (2010) "Canaries in the Mines: *Significance of Sino-Indian Interaction in Myanmar*" European Institute for Asian Studies, Briefing Papers, Brussels. Accessed on March 1, 2013. URL: http://www.eias.org/sites/default/files/EIAS_Briefing_Papers_February_2010_1.pdf

TOI (2013), "China appoints special envoy to Myanmar", March 13.

U Win (1948), 'United Asia', Magazine of Bombay, July 7, pp. 66. Quoted in R.L. Soni, (1955), *The Cultural Study of Burmese Era*, Institute of Buddhist Culture, Mandalay, p. 143.

SECTION III

Bilateral Economic Engagements and Technical Cooperation

7
Bilateral Economic Engagement and Economic Cooperation

Cho Cho Thein

The changes in International environment as well as in Myanmar's political economy have been witnessed in the late 1980s. After decades of isolation, Myanmar is now actively re-engaging with the global economy. The government is endeavouring to emerge as a modern, developed and democratic nation that improves the livelihood of its people. The government has high aspirations for people-centred development, while staying focused on achievable results. In this context, Myanmar has embarked on a historic set of reforms to modernize and open up its economy. The government is laying down and implementing reform strategies for sustainable socio-economic development of Myanmar.

Changes in Political Economy of Myanmar

As soon as the new government took office, the successive reforms in politics and economic development have been carried out. The initial stage was political reform in 2011, which placed a great deal of emphasis on undertaking reforms geared towards political liberalization and national reconciliation. The government has made peace agreements with most of ethnic minorities and armed groups. Besides, the institutional reforms have also made progress by issuing new labour laws to allow union and strikes and by establishing National Human Rights Commission.

Regarding the socio-economic development, the second phase of reform strategy started in June 2012. The foreign investment law has been promulgated to attract foreign investments in the country, as Myanmar was insufficient in capital, technology and human resources, despite its richness in natural resources. The government will adopt a 'people-centred approach' in line with the Framework on Economic and Social Reform (FESR) when reforming the ten priority areas, such as finance and revenue, relaxation of restrictions on trade and foreign investments, development of the private sector, education, health, development of the agricultural sector, food security, transparency in government, the spread in the use of mobile phones and Internet systems and the development of basic infrastructure.

The third phase is to undertake administrative and management reforms. In order to help achieve economic growth and raise the living standards of all citizens, the government is striving to foster *good governance* and promote *clean government* throughout the country.

Due to these successive reforms, the international community has made significant changes in their respective policies towards Myanmar.

To enhance economic development and raise the living standard of Myanmar people, the four economic policies, as guiding principles of Myanmar Comprehensive Development Vision (MCDV[1]), are laid down as follows: (19 June, 2012):

(a) Development of agriculture and all round development;
(b) Balanced and proportionate growth among regions and states;
(c) Inclusive growth for entire population;
(d) Emergence of reliable statistics and improvement of the statistical system.

Under the rule of the democratic government, the Myanmar's economy has been changing significantly. Myanmar is located in a strategic position between the two global giants: China and India. In addition, Myanmar is a land bridge between ASEAN and SAARC.

Table 7.1: Size of Economy

Country	*GDP (USD Mil) in 2011*	*% of World Economy*	*GDP (PPP) (USD Million) in 2011*	*% of World Economy*	*Nominal to PPP Ratio*
Bangladesh	113,855	0.16	283,469	0.36	1: 2.5
Cambodia	12,890	0.02	33,463	0.04	1: 2.6
China	7,298,147	10.44	11,299,987	14.31	1: 1.5
India	1,826,811	2.61	4,420,563	5.60	1: 2.4
Laos	8,302	0.01	17,433	0.02	1: 2.1
Myanmar	51,444	0.07	82,678	0.10	1: 1.6
Thailand	345,672	0.49	602,216	0.76	1: 1.7
Vietnam	122,722	0.18	299,980	0.38	1: 2.4

Source: IMF, WEO Database 2012.

By comparing the sizes of economies among Asian countries, China's GDP is the largest both in absolute terms as well as percentage share in the world economy. India is the second largest economy in Asia. Myanmar, however, is second rank in CLMV countries. According to the advantage of geographic location, Myanmar has a high potentiality to emerge as a modern and developed nation.

Figure 7.1: Structure of Economy (A-I-S Ratio 2011)

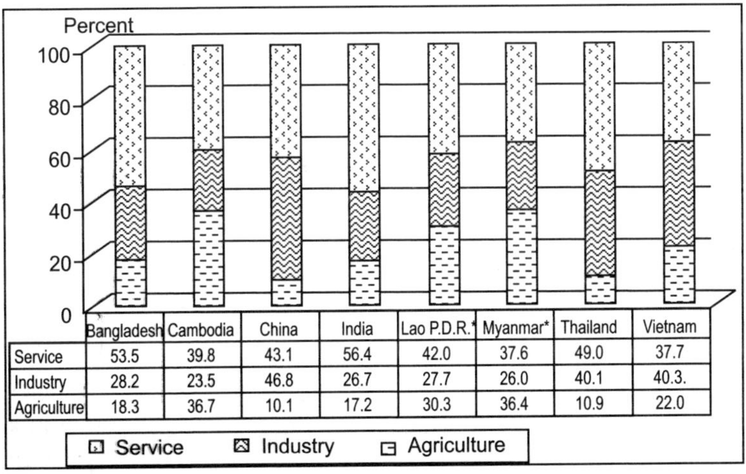

	Bangladesh	Cambodia	China	India	Lao P.D.R.*	Myanmar*	Thailand	Vietnam
Service	53.5	39.8	43.1	56.4	42.0	37.6	49.0	37.7
Industry	28.2	23.5	46.8	26.7	27.7	26.0	40.1	40.3.
Agriculture	18.3	36.7	10.1	17.2	30.3	36.4	10.9	22.0

Service Industry Agriculture

Source: ADB, Key Indicators for Asia and the Pacific 2012.
Note: *2010

As an agro-based economy, the government is paying special emphasis on agricultural development for further cementing the national strength. For the long-term national interest, the government was able to lay down eight rural development and poverty alleviation programmes as a national goal in such a short span of time. According to Figure 7.1, Myanmar needs to catch up with neighbouring agro-based economies. The government has made investments in agricultural development in Myanmar.

By recognizing the lack of capital, technology and human resources against the abundant natural resources, the list of priorities[2] as the driver for economic growth, have been set up as follows: the first on the agenda is to establish labour intensive factories and workshops not only in major towns, but also in smaller townships; the second is the establishment of small and medium size enterprises for the production of value-added goods; the third is to set up heavy industry utilizing Myanmar's own natural resources; and the fourth is to develop information technology in the country.

As national development calls for human resource development, technology and technical expertise, it is necessary to invite foreign direct investments, as the country is in need of capital. Thus, legal framework and the rule of law, infrastructural development incentives, political stability, competitiveness with neighbours, environmental and social accountability are to be reinforced to be able to invite investment.

Because of the lack of capital, the external debt of Myanmar in 2010 was about 14.8 per cent of the gross national income.[3] The government is seeking ways to reduce the burden of national debt by seeking bridge loans and clearing the outstanding debts due to ADB, World Bank and Japan International Cooperation Agency, following the Paris Club creditor countries' cancellation of 50 per cent of the total arrears due to them. Regarding the development assistance, World Bank has contributed US$ 80 million towards community-driven project to be implemented over a period of six years from 2012 to 2019. "Staff Monitoring programme" of IMF has also provided framework for economic cooperation between IMF and the government of Myanmar to use the debt relief and fresh loans for infrastructure development and poverty alleviation programme effectively. Apart from the financial and technical assistance of ADB, World Bank and IMF, the government is making successful coordination with major donor countries, development partners and neighbouring countries.

India-Myanmar Relations

As far as international relations are concerned, relations between Myanmar and India are long and historic. Myanmar is a bridge between India and Southeast Asian markets, and India's gateway to Southeast Asia. Geographical proximity between India and Myanmar has translated into long-standing economic and commercial relations between the two countries both across the land and sea routes. India-Myanmar bilateral trade had grown steadily since late 1990s. According to Indo-Myanmar Trade Agreement, trade between India and Myanmar can be done in three ways: conventional trade, border trade and normal trade. The bartering of local products is permitted for citizens from both countries staying within 40 kilometres from the borders for up to US$ 1000 according to the Grievances Redressal (GR) procedures. Barter trade is permitted for 22 items up to US$ 20,000 in value as per the procedure of Director General of Foreign Trade. Normal trade can be operated with Letter of Credit (LoC) according to export/import policy. From fiscal year 2007-2008 to 2010-2012, the normal trade volume has increased yearly, except slight decrease in the fiscal year 2010-2011. The trade balance has always been in favour of Myanmar and bilateral trade volume with India was the second biggest for Myanmar in its total trade volume with other countries. India is the biggest trading partner of Myanmar after China, among non-ASEAN countries.

Major export items from Myanmar to India are beans, pluses, teak, hard wood, forestry products, raw leather and rubber. Primary imports from India are pharmaceuticals, construction items, machineries, tyres and tubes, plastic goods, iron and steel, electricity distribution equipments, chemicals and fertilizers. The total normal trade volume between Myanmar and India was US$ 1037.116 million in 2011-2012. The bilateral trade between India and Myanmar is expected to touch US$ 3 billion by 2015, on account of healthy growth in the past few years.

Regarding development of border trade, the agreement for Myanmar-India border trade had been made on 21 January 1994 to operate official trading with Myanmar and India under the market economy system. Official trading was made operational by opening Tamu border trade on 12 April 1995 and Rhi border trade on 10th December 2001. Through the Moreh-Tamu border trade region, the goods are distributed through Imphal to Kohima.

For the convenience of trade between Myanmar and India, India will take the responsibility to upgrade/repair 71 bridges on the Tamu-Kalewa road. Moreover, negotiation had been made to upgrade the route of Kalay-Kalewa-Yargyi-Monywa to highway road before 2016. The Kalewa-Yargyi sector will be constructed by India and Yargyi-Monywa sector by Myanmar. Trilateral highway project from Moreh in India to Mae-sot in Thailand will run through Myanmar connecting the three countries. As relationship between citizens play an important role in connecting two countries, it was decided to start the bus service between Imphal in India to Mandalay in Myanmar.

Regarding tax and duties, India collects export tax of one per cent. Less export tax encourages high export volume from India. The custom department of India does not collect duties for the commodities from the third countries; rather, they are confiscated. The custom department of India pays about Rupees 27 million per year to the Central Government.

In the Myanmar-India border trade, at the Moreh-Tamu border, trade volume in the fiscal year 2010-11 was US$ 6.173 million and in 2011-12, it was US$ 6.948 million. Therefore, trade volume of US$ 0.775 million more was exported than the previous year. For Rhi-Tiddim border trade, the trade volume in the fiscal year 2010-11 was US$ 6.628 million and in 2011-12, it was US$ 7.851 million. As a result, trade volume US$ 1.223 million more was exported than the previous year. The major commodities of Myanmar-India border trade include 85 per cent of China products, five per cent of Thailand

and ten per cent of Myanmar. Myanmar exports betel, iced-fish, dried-fish, pork, turmeric root, China exports Meer blanket, soap, snacks, apples and Rauwolfia; whereas India exports wheat, fertilizer, spare parts, wheels, sewing machines, pharmaceuticals and indigenous medicine to Myanmar. Even though Myanmar wishes to import more fertilizers, that is a restricted commodity from India. So is wheat, which is a restricted commodity from Myanmar, which India wishes to export more to Myanmar. For boosting trade and fighting against illegal trade, mobile teams are undertaking inspection tours in each border trade route.

Bilateral relations and cooperation between Myanmar and India continues to enhance due to reciprocal visits of Leaders from both countries. During the official visit of the Prime Minister of India to Myanmar, a MoU was signed for US$ 500 million loan to the country. These loans are to be utilized for the development of infrastructure, agriculture, railway, electric power, development of border areas and to open more border markets.

India and Myanmar signed four economic cooperation agreements, demonstrating the expanding partnership between the two countries. The first agreement is the Bilateral Investment Promotion Agreement (BIPA) between the two governments designed to facilitate greater Indian investment in Myanmar and vice versa. The second agreement is a credit line agreement between the Exim Bank of India and the Myanmar Foreign Trade Bank for US$ 64 million for financing three 230 kv transmission lines in Myanmar to be executed by the Power Grid Corporation of India. The third agreement is a credit line agreement between the Exim Bank of India and the Myanmar Trade Bank for US$ 20 million for financing the establishment of an aluminium conductor steel reinforced (ACSR) wire manufacturing facility to be used for the expansion of the power distribution network in Myanmar. The fourth agreement is between the United Bank of India and the Myanmar Economic Bank for providing banking arrangement for the implementation of the border trade agreement between the two governments that took place at Moreh (in Manipur).

Moreover, Kaldan Multi-Modal Transit Transportation Project (KMMTT)[4] is very important for Myanmar-India trade route. It will help in the development of infrastructure and economic development in both countries. The total outlay for that project is estimated to be about US$ 500 million. If the Kaladan project is finished, commodities from landlocked regions of India can be sent to Sittwe through Kaladan River passing through the Chin state. These commodities can also be exported to other Southeast Asian countries. Local entrepreneurs and merchants will have a chance to cooperate in economic affairs with international entrepreneurs. The Rakhine state will have a chance to export marine products to the international market.

The construction of Sittwe Port will support the economic development of Rakhine and Chin State of Myanmar and will enhance the volume of commodity flow between Myanmar and India. It will also lift the social and economic status of the local ethnic people of that region. Before the connection from Kolkata, India to Mizoram, Aizawl (length 1967 km), however it can shorten by 673 km after Sittwe Project is finished. India plans to construct a 248 km long road from Myanmar-India border to Sittwe in Myanmar and 157 km waterway from Sittwe to Paletwa. The Kaladan Multi-Modal Transit Transport Project will promote trade and communication between both countries, in addition to supporting the development of social life of northeastern region of India.

As a whole, Myanmar is located at the central point of South, Southeast and East Asia; and it is the second largest neighbouring country of India, located near the Bay of Bengal. A strategic country between India and China, Myanmar will have access to both land and normal trade with both countries. Normal trade as well as border trade are playing pivotal role in the bilateral economic relations between the two countries. To foster the trade relations, there are some chokepoints in border trade check points.

Myanmar traders prefer payment in advance for the transactions of goods between the two countries. In 2008, India and Myanmar signed an agreement to conduct payment of traded goods through Myanmar state-owned banks, Myanmar Foreign Trade Bank (MFTB), Myanmar Investment and Commercial Bank (MICB) and United

Bank of India (UBI). However, this procedure could not be implemented effectively, as transfer of payment for traded goods is conducted through Singapore, which increases the cost of trade between the two countries.

Way Ahead

Since for trade facilitation, logistic network is needed, which is less developed between India and Myanmar, there is a need to speed up the infrastructure projects for border trade development. There is a need to cooperate with SMEs to gain capital and technology for extending market and producing quality products. As the sanctions have been lifted and relaxed, there is a good opportunity for Myanmar and entrepreneurs to engage for the economic development. One of the political objectives was to build a modern and developed state according to the Constitution. Regarding the engagement of neighbouring country, the border trade is a driving force for the development of border areas between the two countries. Border trade can increase public-to-public relationship more closely and can lessen border disputes and racial problems. Economic engagements and technical cooperation is based upon complementarities and helps maximize the mutual benefits of all involved. As part of the BIMESTC, BCIM, MGCs and ASEAN, regional integration can produce win-win outcomes in both quantity and quality of economic growth for mutual benefits.

To promote bilateral trade and commercial relations, India and Myanmar should work in close cooperation. The two countries need to continue interacting on Track I and Track II forums, like Delhi Dialogue, for sharing information and ideas.

Conclusion

Changes in macro-economic environment of Myanmar (such as relaxation of economic sanctions by western countries, revising FDI Law, establishing special economic zones: Dawei Sea Port, SMEs policy) are very obvious and have created sound environment for foreign investors and development partners. In that context, and more generally, efforts to enhance coordination are welcome in support of more effective collaboration with Myanmar in the following areas: poverty alleviation programme as development partners, to develop the border trade relations and border regions as strategic partners, infrastructure development projects for regional connectivity, capacity building programmes for Human Resource Development and training/seminar for technical knowhow to help in the catching-up process.

Economic cooperation and integration is based upon complementarities and helps maximize the mutual benefits of all involved. By working together, both countries enjoy social and economic benefits that may not occur through individual efforts alone. Regional integration can produce win-win outcomes in both the quantity and quality of economic growth.

REFERENCES

1. Myanmar Comprehensive Development Vision (MCDV) is "a long-term development aspiration and a set of growth strategies, which provide the foundation for a comprehensive and consistent set of economic policies, infrastructure and HRD plans, industrial sector-wise growth paths, Region and State development master plans and so forth."
2. New Light of Myanmar (16.2.2013).
3. ADB Key Inidacator for Asia and Pacific 2012.
4. The MoU between the government of Myanmar and India, to construct the road from Paletwa to Mizoram Region of North-east India in the Sittwe Deep Sea Port project was signed on 2nd April, 2008.

8
India-Myanmar Economic Relations

Sanjay Pulipaka

Myanmar has witnessed rapid political changes in the recent past. President Thein Sein government, which came to power after 2010 elections, initiated wide ranging political reforms. Aung San Suu Kyi, after her release from house-arrest, contested the recent by-elections (April 2012) and emerged victorious. Suu Kyi's National League for Democracy (NLD) won landslide victory in the by-elections winning 43 out of 45 seats. As a consequence of all these developments, Myanmar, which was treated as an international pariah till recently by many countries, witnessed a flurry of visits from various heads of the state. Many countries are calling for greater engagement with Myanmar. In May 2012, the Indian Prime Minister Manmohan Singh held wide-ranging consultations with people from across the political spectrum (President Thein Sein and also with opposition leader Aung San Suu Kyi) during his visit to Myanmar. The governments of both countries have identified priority areas to enhance relations between the two countries. In the light of these developments, this chapter gives a very brief history of India-Myanmar relations, explores India's economic engagement and juxtaposes it with policies adopted by a few others towards Myanmar.

A Brief History of India-Myanmar Relations

India and Myanmar have strong historical ties. The spread of Buddhism from India to Myanmar and vibrant cultural interactions have often been referred to demonstrate the strong historical ties between the two countries. However, history also gives some unwanted baggage. It was during the British colonial times that India and Myanmar (then Burma) had intense interactions. Myanmar was one of the provinces of British India till 1937. The common state apparatus and the economic policies of the colonial masters prompted significant movement of Indian population into Myanmar. The British consciously brought in people from India to man the administrative positions in Myanmar. For instance in 1938, 71 per cent of civil police force were Bamar, Indians and Karens constituted 11.5 per cent and 8.7 per cent, respectively.[1] On the other hand, in Yangon, while 67 per cent of civil police force were Indians, the Bamars constituted only about 26 per cent.[2] Over time, people of Indian origin emerged as important players in the economy. Myanmar had substantial presence of People of Indian Origin (PIOs) before the Second World War.[3] According to the 1931 Census, the number of Indians in Burma was at 10,17,825.[4] The exact figures during the colonial period are not certain as many may have listed themselves under the category 'Burmese speaking'.[5] Therefore, by 1940, the number of PIOs would have been way above the numbers suggested. The perception among the local Burmese that their employment and business opportunities are shrinking because of the presence of the 'outsiders' laid the foundation for the emergence of xenophobic tendencies, which impacted India-Myanmar relations to a significant extent for a considerable period of time.

Cooperation: Infant States and Nation-Building

During the early years of independence, Myanmar was beset by insurgency and the writ of the government was often confined to the capital city of Yangon. It was during those trying times that India extended assistance to the then government of Myanmar. Reportedly, India and Burma contemplated the possibility of security treaty in 1950.[6] Instead, both the countries signed a Treaty of Friendship in 1951, which stated that "there shall be everlasting peace and unalterable friendship between the two States."[7] During the early years after independence, there was also some, if not complete, similarity in the foreign policy approaches of both the countries. For instance, both countries followed the policy of Non-Alignment. The overthrow of democratic government and emergence of military dictatorship in 1962 was a source of discomfiture for India. Further, the Burminisation policies (Burmese Way to Socialism) contributed to the growing unease in India. Nationalisation/Burmanisation policies of General Ne Win resulted in forced migration of substantial number of PIOs from Myanmar. These policies did indeed generate stress in the relationship between India and Myanmar. There was also growing divergence in the foreign policies of the two countries. Interestingly, Myanmar withdrew from Non-Aligned Movement (NAM) in 1979, as it felt that the NAM was moving closer to the Soviet bloc. Myanmar's foreign minister at the Sixth NAM Conference in Cuba observed that "the principles of the movement are not recognizable anymore: they are not merely dim, but they are dying.[8]" However, the relationship between the two countries did not witness significant change, as there were regular meetings at various levels. The necessity to address the raging insurgencies in the Northeast India and in northern Myanmar prompted the leadership on both sides to stay engaged.

Negotiating Regime Differences

During the late 1980s and early 1990s, India strongly supported the movement for democracy in Myanmar. Referring to the pro-democracy student protest, the Indian Ministry of External Affairs statement reportedly stated: "Undaunted resolve of the Burmese [Myanmar] people to achieve their democracy…. be able to fulfil their legitimate aspirations for a representative government."[9] The elections of 1990 and the reluctance of the then government of Myanmar to recognize the electoral verdict contributed to the friction between the two governments. Further, Aung San Suu Kyi was given the Jawaharlal Nehru Award in 1993, demonstrating India's support for the democracy movement in Myanmar. However, it appears that there was some recalibration in India's policy from as early as 1992.

In 1992, U Aye, a senior official of the Burmese Foreign Ministry, visited India and in 1993 J.N. Dixit, Indian Foreign Secretary, visited Myanmar.[10] These visits laid the foundation for India's foreign policy changes and since the mid-1990s, India adopted a more nuanced approach in its relations with Myanmar because of security, ethnic, economic and geopolitical considerations. Gradually, the relationship acquired a certain comfort level and it became possible for India to envisage enhanced economic interactions and connectivity projects involving Myanmar.

India-Myanmar Economic Relations

It would not be an exaggeration to say that India's economic engagement of Myanmar has been less than satisfactory. According to statistics compiled by the European Union, India is the third largest trading partner of Myanmar. However, a closer look at the figures will reveal the absence of diversity in Myanmar's international trade and also India's weak trade-links with Myanmar. China and Thailand account for 31.4 per cent and 28.8 per cent of Myanmar's international trade, respectively. This implies that China and Thailand account for more than 60 per cent of Myanmar's international trade. On the other hand, India's trade with Myanmar is a mere 7.6 per cent of the latter's overall trade. It should be noted that because of problems associated with the official exchange rates of the Myanmar Kyat, a large component of India-Myanmar trade is conducted through Singapore, which does not get reflected in the official trade figures. Nonetheless, the overall trade between India and Myanmar is way below its potential. This despite the fact that India shares approximately 1643 km of land border with Myanmar (four Indian states share border with Myanmar) and for India, Myanmar is a critical land-bridge to Southeast Asia. While India imports edible vegetables, wood and wood products, it exports pharmaceutical products, electrical and electronic equipment and machinery.[11] Significantly, India imports pulses from Myanmar in large quantities and such imports account for as much as 33 per cent of India's global imports of edible vegetables.[12]

State	*Total Length (Km)*
Arunachal Pradesh	520
Nagaland	215
Manipur	398
Mizoram	510
Total	1643

Source: Management of Indo-Myanmar Border, Report of Ministry of Home Affairs, Government of India, available at http://mha.nic.in/pdfs/BM_MAN-IN-MYAN(E).pdf

Figure 8.1

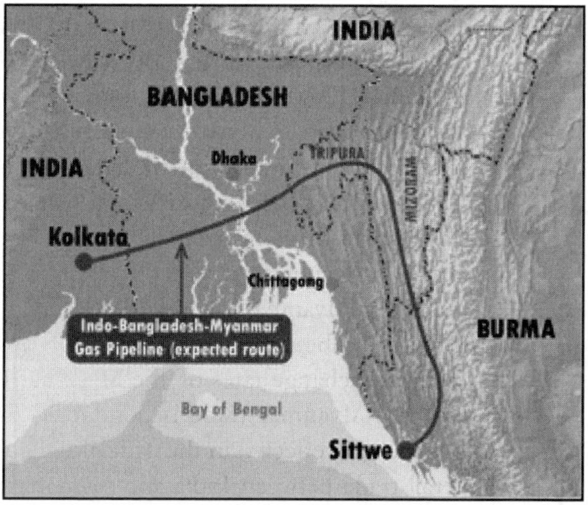

Source: Louis Reh, "Daewoo Urged to Quit Arakan Gas Field Project," The Irrawaddy, 14 October 2005, available at http://www2.irrawaddy.org/article.php?art_id=5093

In spite of geographic contiguity, India's border trade with Myanmar is insufficiently developed and imbalanced. India and Myanmar signed a border trade agreement in 1994, which mandates that the trade between the two will take place through Customs Posts in Moreh (India) -Tamu (Myanmar) and Zowkhathar (India) -Rhi

(Myanmar).[13] With only two border trade points (Moreh-Tamu, Zokhawthar-Rhi) currently functional, it is not surprising that India's formal border trade with Myanmar is meager, amounting to less than one per cent of the overall India-Myanmar trade.[14] Informal border trade, reported to be in the region of approximately US$ 11 million a month, is also conducted across the porous border.[15] However, the prevailing security situation, informal taxes by insurgent groups,[16] and absence of road and rail connectivity networks, tend to hinder greater border trade between the two countries.

Energy Requirements

To meet domestic energy requirements, India was very keen on accessing the natural resources of Myanmar, such as the natural gas. According to Marie Lall, ensuring priorities played a significant role in determining India's policy towards Myanmar, as she observed: "India's domestic energy priorities are so urgent that it is willing to go ahead with the pipeline, no matter what the wider world says. In many ways, this disapproval will be seen as a small price to pay for

Figure 8.2

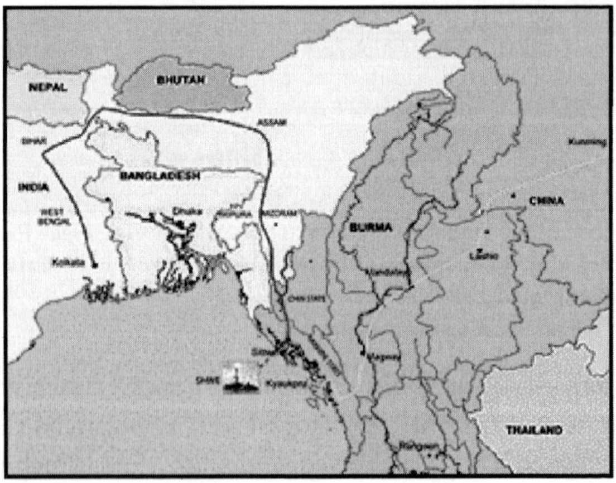

Source: "Burma Human Rights Year Book 2006," Report of National Coalition Government of the Union of Burma (NCGUB), 2006 http://www.ncgub.net/NCGUB/BHRY/2006/labour.html

what are a range of solutions to immediate issues. Besides, in today's volatile international relations environment where nations fall in and out of favour, Myanmar's pariah position might well be seen as temporary.[17]"

It was in 2004 that a consortium consisting of Daewoo, Korea Gas Corporation (KOGAS), Oil & Natural Gas Corporation, India (ONGC), Myanmar Oil and Gas Enterprise (MOGE), Gas Authority of India (GAIL) announced that they discovered "world-class commercial-scale gas deposit" of over five trillion cubic feet (tcf) at the Shwe gas field.[18] Given the domestic energy requirements, India was very keen to access these natural gas deposits and explore the possibility of putting in a pipeline from the Shwe gas field. India-Bangladesh-Myanmar pipeline agreement was reached in 2005 according to which Bangladesh was to receive US$ 125 million in annual transit fees.[19] However, Bangladesh placed numerous conditions, such as free trade corridor to Nepal, removal of trade barriers, purchase of hydro-power from Bhutan and so on.[20] For India, such extraneous conditionalities for operationalizing the pipeline were difficult to accept. As an India's Ministry of External Affairs official reportedly observed: "Under no circumstances should India accept any of the (Bangladesh's) conditions... That will encourage Dhaka to tie up unrelated conditionalities in future negotiations on other issues, as it is always prone to do. India will always consider bonafide demands from Bangladesh, but they cannot start unfair bargaining."[21] Given the difficulties of roping in Bangladesh, India explored the possibility of putting a pipeline through Indian territory (Northeast India) completely avoiding Bangladesh. While India was still figuring its way through in identifying the best possible route for the pipeline, Myanmar agreed to sell the natural gas from Shwe Gas Fields (A-1, A-3) to China in late 2008. Compared to other bidders, such as India, while China may be paying less for the natural gas,[22] China's veto power, its status as steady supplier of arms and its unwillingness to criticize the government of Myanmar on democracy and human rights issues, seems to have clinched the deal.

Along with exploring the possibility of establishing energy pipelines, India has been working on improving its connectivity networks with Myanmar, to improve overall economic activity and the following are some of the significant projects underway:

Kaladan Multi-Modal Project

The Kaladan Multi-Modal Project was conceptualized to provide landlocked Northeast India with an access to the sea. More importantly, given the past unpredictability in India's relations with Bangladesh and the problems associated with the absence of transit agreements, the Kaladan multi-modal project was designed to provide alternative transportation networks between India and its landlocked Northeast India. The Kaladan project significantly reduces the distance between major India cities, such as Kolkata and Northeast India. The project also facilitates greater economic interaction between Northeast India, Myanmar and beyond. The project has three components:[23] (a) developing the Sittwe port to facilitate sea transport between Kolkata and Sittwe (539 Kilometers); (b) developing the inland waterway transport between Sittwe to Setpyitpyin (Kaletwa), which is about 225 km; and (c) Setpyitpyin to India-Myanmar border road transport, which is about 62 km.

In April 2008, India and Myanmar signed an agreement on the Kaladan Multi-Modal Project. Two years later, in April 2010, Essar India Ltd was awarded the contract for port construction and for inland water works.[24] The project is facing numerous challenges, such as underestimation of road length and the absence of effective inter-ministerial coordination. The Indian Ministry of Power's proposals to construct hydro-electric projects on tributaries of the Kaladan River have raised concerns about the navigability of the river in the coming years.[25] The joint statement issued during Prime Minister Manmohan Singh's visit to Myanmar in May 2012 "expressed satisfaction at the steady progress being made on the Kaladan Multi-modal Transit Transport Project.[26]" It is anticipated that the construction work pertaining to Sittwe port will be completed by 2013,[27] but there is no clear timeline yet for the project completion.

Trilateral Highway

A Trilateral Ministerial Meeting on Transport Linkages, held in Yangon in April 2002, conceptualized the idea of a Trilateral Highway connecting India, Myanmar and Thailand.[28] The project proposed to link Moreh (India) with Mae Sot (Thailand) through Bagan (Myanmar). In May 2002, providing details of the project, India's External Affairs Minister stated that the Trilateral Highway would be completed within the timeframe of two years and that two task forces had been constituted to operationalise the project.[29] More than a year later, in December 2003, the Foreign Ministers of India, Myanmar and Thailand met in New Delhi and came up with a three phase implementation process wherein all the parties agreed to strengthen the road networks in their respective countries. As per the minutes of the meeting, India was to complete 78 km of missing links in phase-I, explore the possibility of upgrading an additional 132 km, and prepare project reports for the construction of a bridge and causeway across the Irrawaddy River.[30] However, the project continues to face numerous delays.

During his visit to Myanmar in May 2012, Prime Minister Manmohan Singh stated that India would repair/and upgrade 71 bridges on the Tamu-Kalewa friendship road and also upgrade the Kalewa-Yargyi road segment to highway standard.[31] A new deadline, of 2016, for the completion of the Trilateral Highway and the revival of the India-Myanmar-Thailand Joint Task Force was also announced during the visit. The Joint Task Force at its meeting in September 2012 decided to work on issues, such as the harmonization of customs and immigration procedures at border check-posts in order to establish connectivity by 2016.[32]

Stillwell Road

The other major project pertaining to India-Myanmar connectivity is the Stillwell Road, which was constructed during the Second World War to connect Ledo in Assam with Kunming in the Yunnan province of China. Concerns have been expressed in India that the revival of this road would give an advantage to China in the event of hostilities.

Moreover, there are also concerns in Myanmar that the road currently passes through territories controlled by various insurgent groups[33] and hence the revival of this road would result in increased revenues for the armed groups.

Air Connectivity

While the demands for seamless road connectivity between India and Myanmar have to constantly negotiate concerns related to security and terrain, there are no such concerns with regard to air connectivity; yet, the airline connectivity between the two countries is minimal with the operation of only two direct flights a week from India. Proposals from private Indian carriers to start new services to Yangon are yet to materialize. Many in Myanmar complain that while they are very keen on accessing India's health care facilities, they are not able to do so due to the absence of frequent direct air-flights between the two countries. Improvement of air connectivity remains an urgent requirement for enhancing economic ties and people-to-people contacts.

Rail Connectivity

At the moment, rail connectivity between India and Myanmar is completely absent. In 2005, India's RITES Ltd conducted a feasibility study and suggested new rail links between Jiribam-Imphal-Moreh (in India) and Tamu (Moreh)-Kalay-Segyi (in Myanmar).[34] In October 2012, the Indian Cabinet's Committee on Infrastructure approved the construction of a new broad-gauge line from Imphal Road (Tupul) to Imphal at a cost of approximately US$ 822.96 million, to be completed in 2016. The project is facing numerous challenges, such as heavy monsoons, a fragile security situation, and economic blockades. These new rail links would eventually be integrated into the proposed trans-Asian railway project, which seeks to connect Malaysia, Thailand, Vietnam, Cambodia, Myanmar, Bangladesh, India and Pakistan by rail networks.[35]

Border Area Development

During the Indian Prime Minister's visit to Myanmar in May 2012, both sides agreed to start a bus service between Imphal in India and Mandalay in Myanmar and to undertake joint border area development through physical and social infrastructure programmes.

Ports and Integrated Production Networks

Organizations such as the Economic Research Institute for ASEAN and East Asia (ERIA), have been advocating new connectivity networks by operationalizing deep sea ports, such as Dawei in Myanmar, which would provide greater connectivity with the Chennai port in India and beyond. The extended Dawei-Chennai link, termed the Mekong-India Economic Corridor (MIEC) by ERIA, seeks to facilitate integrated production networks between India and ASEAN by combining physical connectivity with industrial clusters and high-speed rail networks. It should be noted that along with Dawei, a fairly large number of ports, such as Yangon, Sittwe, Kyaukphyu, Thandwe, Pathein, Mawlamyine, Myiek, and Kawthaung, are either being constructed or upgraded to handle greater volumes of traffic. It is important for India to quickly expand its port facilities along the eastern seaboard and establish strong linkages along the lines suggested by ERIA, starting with major up-gradation of the Chennai and Ennore ports.

In the recent past, the Indian business community has started investing in Myanmar. In 2010, Tata Motors entered into collaboration with Myanmar Automobile & Diesel Industries Ltd. (MADI) to construct a heavy truck assembly plant in Magwe in central Myanmar.[36] The plant has now been operationalized and Tata Motors is expanding its footprint in Myanmar by entering into a distribution agreement with Apex Greatest Industrial Co. Ltd. (AGI), Myanmar, for the distribution of commercial vehicles and passenger cars in Myanmar.[37]

A large contingent of Indian business persons accompanied the Prime Minister of India to Myanmar in May 2012. During the visit, Jubilant Oil & Gas Private Limited, India, which had acquired onshore natural gas blocks in the Irrawaddy delta in 2011, entered into a

Production Sharing Contract (PSC) with Parami Energy Development Company Limited (Parami) and Myanma Oil & Gas Enterprise (MOGE). Since the Prime Minister's visit, the Indian company, JK Paper, entered into an MU with Myanmar's state owned Thar Paung Paper and Pulp Mill to pick up equity and also to operate, expand and export the product from the mill.[38] It should be noted that in the coming years, Indian companies will have to face intense competition not only from Chinese firms, but also from Japanese, Korean and western firms eager to explore opportunities in the natural resource rich Myanmar economy.

China's Growing Presence

Sanctions by Western countries prompted Myanmar to move closer to China for political and economic support. China seized the opportunity and made rapid in-roads in the political and economic landscape of Myanmar. China expanded its connectivity projects in Myanmar to bolster economic activity in its Yunnan province. More importantly, for China, Myanmar is a natural land-bridge to access the Bay of Bengal and the Indian Ocean. The most ambitious among these projects has been the oil and gas pipelines from Kyaukphyu in the Rakhine province of Myanmar, on the Bay of Bengal coast, to Kunming in the Yunnan province in China.

In 2008, China National Petroleum Corporation (CNPC) signed a contract to import natural gas from the Shwe gas fields in the Bay of Bengal and started the construction of oil and gas pipelines in 2010. It has been reported that the natural gas pipeline, which has the capacity to carry 12 billion cubic meters of gas annually, will be operational by 30 May 2013 and the crude oil pipeline will be operationalized next year.[39] More recently, China Railways Engineering Corporation and the Myanmar Union Ministry of Rail Transportation signed an MoU in 2011 to build the railway network from Kyakphyu to Kunming.[40] China has also operationalized a host of connectivity projects, specifically in Northern Myanmar, which are facilitating deeper economic integration of Myanmar with the bordering regions of China.

China's economic activity and connectivity networks in Myanmar have made its presence in the Bay of Bengal a growing reality, which will have strategic implications in the long run. It appears that Beijing has more ambitious plans for the Bay of Bengal, including a special economic zone, power plants and a deep water commercial seaport in Kyaukphyu, involving up to US$ 100 billion in investment in the coming years.[41] Given the scope of such investments, strategist C. Raja Mohan asks, "Would it be illogical, then, for Beijing to consider securing its massive investments in Kyaukpyu with a credible naval presence in the Bay of Bengal?[42]" It should also be noted that China already possesses significant leverage in terms of the relationship it has with some of the armed ethnic groups on Myanmar's northeastern borders.[43]

China is by far the largest investor in Myanmar. The Chinese investments (including investments from Hong Kong) amounted to US$ 20 billion in 2012, which was approximately half of the total US$ 41 billion FDI in Myanmar during 1989-2012.[44] Its only setback in recent years has been the suspension of the Myitsone hydro-power project on the Irrawaddy River, on account of widespread popular discontent over population displacement, environmental impact and the sale of bulk of the power generated to China.

Growing Engagement of Japan, Thailand and Others

In the past, Japan's trade and investment with Myanmar were constrained by economic sanctions and the autarkic economic policies of the Myanmar regime. During the period 1988-2010, Japan accounted for less than one per cent of international investment in Myanmar. In the past two years, Japan has been making sustained efforts to scale up its engagement. Japan's trade with Myanmar has registered a significant increase, with exports doubling to US$ 492 million in 2010.[45] There is anticipation that Japanese investments will also witnesses significant increase as infrastructure deficiencies are resolved. Japan has waived US$ 3.7 billion of US$ 6 billion in debt owed to it by Myanmar.[46] Further, the Japan Bank for International Cooperation has provided Myanmar with a bridging loan of US$ 900 million to pay off some of its debt to the World Bank and the Asian Development Bank.[47] Japanese financial institutions such as the Mitsubishi UFJ Financial Group Inc. will be playing an important role in disbursing Japan's financial assistance and are seeking to collaborate with local entities, such as Myanmar's Co-Operative Bank Ltd.[48] Japan is also actively involved in developing urban infrastructure facilities, such as water supply and sewage systems in Yangon, under Japan's International Cooperation Agency (JICA) financing.[49]

Japan's Deputy Prime Minister and Finance Minister, Taro Aso, visited Myanmar in January 2013, which was the first overseas visit by a senior cabinet minister after Shinzo Abe's Liberal Democratic Party (LDP) government took office. The visit signalled the importance of Myanmar in Japan's Southeast Asian policy. Aso visited the site of the Thilawa Special Economic Zone, reiterating Japan's commitment to large scale industrial infrastructure projects in Myanmar. The Thilawa project has been termed as the "centre-piece of Japan's investment in Myanmar" and it comprises a 2,400-hectare special economic zone and an industrial park with an estimated cost of US$ 12.6 billion, which will include a 500 megawatt power plant at a cost of US$ 900 million.[50]

Similarly, Thailand has been keen to develop the Dawei Special Economic Zone (SEZ) in the Tanintharyi Region of Myanmar. When the Dawei project ran into financial trouble, Thailand invited Japan to become a partner in the development of Dawei SEZ.[51] Reportedly, Japan has already extended support for the project by advancing soft loans, which would be used for the construction of port and road infrastructure.[52] This indicates that the countries in the region are comfortable with Japan's growing economic engagement in Myanmar, which is aimed at integrating Myanmar with production networks of Southeast Asia.

Thailand is the second largest investor in Myanmar with an estimated investment of some US$ 7.41 billion during 1998-2009.[53] A significant component (approx. 80-90%) of Thailand's investment has been in the energy sector.[54] Thailand's state owned Energy Company PTT, which has already made significant investments, is planning to invest an additional US$ 3 billion in Myanmar.[55]

The other major player in Myanmar's economic landscape is South Korea, which is the fourth largest investor. While companies such as Daewoo have been operating in the energy sector, South Korean companies are now seeking to diversify their investment portfolio by investing in sectors such as communications, vehicles and auto parts and mining.[56]

Finally, with the suspension/lifting of sanctions, companies from the West are actively exploring investment opportunities in Myanmar. While companies, such as Chevron and Total have been operating for some time, others such as British Petroleum and Royal Dutch Shell are considering investments in Myanmar.[57] To distribute its products in Myanmar, PepsiCo has signed an agreement with Diamond Star Co., Ltd., and is also exploring investments in the agricultural sector.[58] In the coming months and years, there is going to be intense competition among various international actors to gain economic leverage in resource rich Myanmar.

Late mover's disadvantage, difficult terrain and differences in administrative and political cultures have been some of the reasons for delays in Indian projects in Myanmar. Nonetheless, it would be no exaggeration to state that these delays in connectivity projects are costing India not only economically, but also in terms of political and social goodwill. Expeditious implementation of connectivity projects between India and Southeast Asian countries starting with Myanmar is today a strategic imperative for the success of the LEP.

Conclusion

As India scaled up its engagement with Myanmar, there was growing criticism that India has bartered its principles at the altar of realist approach. For instance, Senior General Than Shwe's visit to India in July 2010 evoked sharp reaction from the United States. The US State Department spokesman said, "Others, who have relationships with Burma, share a responsibility to communicate directly and forcefully to Burma about its responsibilities, whether they are protecting the region against the risk of proliferation or telling Burma directly that it should more constructively engage with its opposition and other ethnic groups within Burma.[59]" In the recent past, Indian and Chinese engagements with Myanmar have come under intense scrutiny. Both countries have been criticised for not pushing the then government of Myanmar to speed up the transition process. The scale of Indian engagement may not match the Chinese engagement and at the same time, more importantly, the nature of the Indian engagement in Myanmar is also qualitatively different from that of China. India's engagement with Myanmar has been multidimensional. It should be noted that India has been actively engaging Myanmar in the realms of education and business training. The Indian engagement has been aimed at enhancing the capacities of many youngsters to access the fruits of development. For instance, India has set up a host of institutions, such as Myanmar India Entrepreneurial Development Centre, India Myanmar Industrial Training Centre, and Myanmar Centre for English Training. These institutions are working to enhance the capacities of the citizens of Myanmar in various fields, such as entrepreneurship and basic skills required for industrial growth among other areas. Moreover, in the recent past, India has been training journalists from Myanmar, which very few neighbouring countries of Myanmar can claim credit for. If India's policy towards Myanmar has to be faulted, then it should not be on the content. Rather, the criticism should focus on the scale of operations and the speed with which it works.

REFERENCES

1. Robert H. Taylor, *The State in Myanmar*, London: Foundation Books, p. 102.
2. *Ibid.*
3. The Indian population in Myanmar registered a decrease in 1960s due to General Ne Win's nationalisation policy.
4. John L. Christian, "Burma," *Annals of the American Academy of Political and Social Science*, Vol. 226, March 1943, pp. 120-121.
5. *Ibid.*
6. C Raja Mohan, "The Return of Treaty Diplomacy," *Centre for Policy Research.* Available http://www.cprindia.org/blog/foreign-policy/3582-return-treaty-diplomacy.

7. For the text of the treaty see, Treaty of Friendship Between India and the Union of Burma [1951], 7 July 1951. Available http://www.commonlii.org/in/other/treaties/INTSer/1951/12.html.
8. William L. Scully and Frank N. Trager, "Burma 1979: Reversing the Trend," *Asian Survey*, vol. 20, no. 2, (1980), pp. 172-173.
9. Sanjoy Hazarika, "India, Breaking Its Silence, Backs Government Opponents in Burma," *New York Times*, September 13, 1988. Available: http://www.nytimes.com/1988/09/13/world/india-breaking-its-silence-backs-government-opponents-in-burma.html.
10. Soe Myint, India and Burma: Working on Their Relationship, *The Irrawaddy*, vol. 7, no. 3. Available http://www2.irrawaddy.org/print_article.php?art_id=1170
11. "India-Myanmar Relations," *Report of Ministry of External Affairs*, Government of India, May 2012. Available http://www.mea.gov.in/Images/pdf/india-myanmar-relations-24-05-2012-press-release.pdf.
12. "Potential For Enhancing India's Trade with Myanmar: A Brief Analysis," *Report of Export-Import Bank of India*, Working Paper no. 17, April 2012.
13. While there are border trade points such as Avakhung (in Nagaland) and Nampong (in Arunachal Pradesh), infrastructural facilities are very weak. As a consequence, Moreh witnesses relatively more intense border trade.
14. E.Bijoykumar Singh, "NER-Myanmar Border Trade: The Emerging Pattern," *India-Myanmar Border Trade Bulletin*, December 2012, vol. 1, no. 1, p. 17. Available: http://economics.manipuruniv.ac.in/SAP/Bulletine/bulletine.pdf.
15. Pranjal Baruah, "Biz Booms Beyond Borders, *Times of India*, 10 September 2012. Available http://articles.timesofindia.indiatimes.com/2012-09-10/guwahati/33736509_1_india-and-myanmar-border-trade-myanmar-traders.
16. "NSCM (I-M) Demand Hits Manipur Border Trade," *Times of India*, 09 May 2012. Available http://articles.timesofindia.indiatimes.com/2002-05-09/india/27130814_1_vehicle-owners-border-trade-nscn.
17. Marie Lall, "Indo-Myanmar Relations in the Era of Pipeline Diplomacy," *Contemporary Southeast Asia*, 2006, vol. 28, no. 3, p. 426.
18. Julien Levesqu, "Is it the Shwe Gas Reserves Talking? ," *The Indian Express*, 23 October 2007. Available http://www.indianexpress.com/story-print/231217/.
19. Varigonda Kesava Chandra, "The Pipeline That Wasn't: Myanmar-Bangladesh-India Natural Gas Pipeline," 19 April 2012. Available http://ensec.org/index.php?option=com_content&view=article&id=348:india-bangladesh-and-the-myanmar-bangladesh-india-natural-gas-pipeline-how-not-to-achieve-energy-s&catid=123:content&Itemid=389.
20 Anand Kumar, "India-Myanmar Gas pipeline Through Bangladesh-Pipe Dream? ," *South Asia Analysis Group Paper,* 07 January 2005, No. 1216. Available http://www.southasiaanalysis.org/papers13/paper1216.html

21. Anand Kumar, "India-Myanmar Gas Pipeline: With or Without Bangladesh?" *South Asia Analysis Group Paper,* 26 July 2005, no. 1474. Available http://www.southasiaanalysis.org/%5Cpapers15%5Cpaper1474.html.
22. William Boot, "Step on the Gas," The Irrawaddy, July 2007, vol. 15, no. 7. Available http://www2.irrawaddy.org/article.php?art_id=7735&page=1.
23. "The Kaladan Multi-Modal Transit Transport Project." Available http://www.mdoner.gov.in/content/introduction-1.
24. *Ibid.*
25. Sandeep Dikshit, "India-Myanmar Transport Project Hits Roadblock," *The Hindu*, 02 May 2012. Available http://www.thehindu.com/news/national/indiamyanmar-transport-project-hits-roadblock/article3377718.ece.
26. "Joint Statement on the occasion of the visit of Prime Minister of India Dr. Manmohan Singh to Myanmar," *Press Information Bureau*, 28 May 2012. Available http://pib.nic.in/newsite/erelease.aspx?relid=84517.
27. Shrimati Preneet Kaur, "Lok Sabha Unstarred Question No. 4435," *Ministry of External Affairs*, 07 September 2012. Available http://www.mea.gov.in/lok-sabha.htm?dtl/20588/Q4435+Kaladan+Project.
28. "India-Myanmar-Thailand Joint Task Force Meeting on the Trilateral Highway Project," *Ministry of External Affairs*, 11 September 2012. Available: http://www.mea.gov.in/press-releases.htm?dtl/20541/IndiaMyanmarThailand+Joint+Task+Force+Meeting+on+the+Trilateral+Highway+Project.
29. "Minister for External Affairs responds to Q. 0632-Trilateral Highway Project Connecting India," *Ministry of External Affairs*, Government of India, 09 May 2002. Available: http://www.mea.gov.in/rajya-sabha.htm?dtl/9440/Q+0632++Traileteral+Highway+Project+Connecting+India.
30. "Briefing Points for Ministerial Meeting on Trilateral Highway Project among India-Myanmar-Thailand," *Ministry for External Affairs*, GoI, 23 December 2003. Available http://www.mea.gov.in/media-briefings.htm?dtl/4904/Briefing+Points+for+Ministerial+Meeting+on+Trilateral+Highway+Project+among+IndiaMyanmarThailand.
31. "Joint Statement on the occasion of the visit of Prime Minister of India Dr. Manmohan Singh to Myanmar," *Press Information Bureau*, 28 May 2012. Available: http://pib.nic.in/newsite/erelease.aspx?relid=84517
32. "India-Myanmar-Thailand Joint Task Force Meeting on the Trilateral Highway Project," *Ministry of External Affairs*, 11 September 2012. Available: http://www.mea.gov.in/press-releases.htm?dtl/20541/IndiaMyanmarThailand+Joint+Task+Force+Meeting+on+the+Trilateral+Highway+Project.
33. K. Anurag, "Myanmar Obstructs Historic Stillwell Road Project," *Rediff*, 17 June 2009. Available http://news.rediff.com/report/2009/jun/17/myanmar-obstructs-stillwell-road-project.htm.
34. "Rail link with Myanmar," *Press Information Bureau*, Government of India, 16 December 2015. Available: http://pib.nic.in/newsite/erelease.aspx?relid=14310.

35. Sujata Dutta Sachdeva, "Delhi to Hanoi? Possible, says Railways" *Times of India*, 21 September 2003. Available: http://articles.timesofindia.indiatimes.com/2003-09-21/india/27217146_1_railway-line-link-indian-railways.

36. "Tata Motors to Construct Heavy Truck Plant in Myanmar under Government of India's Line of Credit," *Tata*, 22 March 2010. Available http://www.tatamotors.com/media/press-releases.php?id=541.

37. "Tata Motors enters into Distribution Agreement in Myanmar," *Tata*, 28 May 2012. Available: http://www.tata.com/media/releases/inside.aspx?artid=t1uYOf0wd+k=

38. MV Ramsurya, "JK Paper to Pick up Equity Stake in Myanmar Pulp Mill," *The Economic Times*, 04 June 2012. Available: http://articles.economictimes.indiatimes.com/2012-06-04/news/32031854_1_pulp-facility-harshpati-singhania-myanmar-government.

    Please note that the maps in this document may not to be up to the scale.

39. Jamil Anderlini and Gwen Robinson, "China-Myanmar Pipeline to open in May," *Financial Times*, 21 January 2013. Available: http://www.ft.com/intl/cms/s/0/faf733ae-63b6-11e2-af8c-00144feab49a.html#axzz2Ocbo4Lt4

40. "China, Myanmar Sign MoU on Rail Transport Project," *Xinhua*, 28 April 2011. Available: http://www.chinadaily.com.cn/bizchina/2011-04/28/content_12412367.htm

41. C. Raja Mohan, "Bengal's Waters," *The Indian Express*, 26 March 2013. Available: http://www.indianexpress.com/news/bengals-waters/1087084/

42. *Ibid.*

43. Bertil Lintner, "Powers Seek Influence in Burma's Conflict," *YaleGlobal Online*, 18 March 2013.

44. Li Tao, "Sino-Myanmar Trade Provides Huge Investment Chances," *Chain Daily*, 16 January 2013. Available: http://www.chinadaily.com.cn/hkedition/2013-01/16/content_16123034.htm.

45. Yoree Koh, "Japan Inc. Rushes to Myanmar," *Reuters*, 25 August 2012. Available: http://online.wsj.com/article/SB1000142405270230397810457736373 0176850196.html.

46. "Myanmar Debt Load Gets $6 Billion Lighter," *Wall Street Journal*, 28 January 2013. Available: http://online.wsj.com/article/SB10001424127887323375204578269123280919556.html. Also see "Japan to Forgive Myanmar Debt to Support Reform," *The New York Times*, 21 April 2012. Available: http://www.nytimes.com/2012/04/22/world/asia/japan-to-forgive-myanmar-debt-to-speed-development.html

47. "Myanmar and World Bank Sign Deal to Clear Old Debt," *The New York Times*, 27 January 2013. Available: http://www.nytimes.com/2013/01/28/business/global/myanmar-signs-deal-with-world-bank-over-debt.html

48. Andy Sharp, "Japan's Aso Targets Myanmar Markets Amid China Rivalry:

Economy," *Bloomberg*, 03 January 2013. Available: http://www.bloomberg.com/news/2013-01-03/aso-leads-japanese-push-into-myanmar-market-dominated-by-china.html

49. Thomas Fuller, "Long Reliant on China, Myanmar Now Turns to Japan," *The New York Times*, 10 October 2012. Available: http://www.nytimes.com/2012/10/11/world/asia/long-reliant-on-china-myanmar-now-turns-to-japan-for-help.html?pagewanted=all
50. Antoni Slodkowski, "Japan Inc Steals a March in Myanmar," *Reuters*, 03 October 2012. Available: http://graphics.thomsonreuters.com/12/09/JapanMyanmar.pdf
51. "Thailand Urges Japan to Join in Myanmar's Dawei Projects," *Xinhua*, 18 January 2013. Available: http://news.xinhuanet.com/english/world/2013-01/18/c_124246395.htm
52. Nongnapas Maipanit, "Chances High of Japanese Investment in Dawei: Minister," *Eleven*, 19 January 2013. Available: http://elevenmyanmar.com/asean/2169-chances-high-of-japanese-investment-in-dawei-minister. Also see Jason Szep and Amy Sawitta Lefevre, "Japan, Thailand race to rescue of Myanmar's struggling Dawei," *Reuters*, 21 September 2012. Available: http://www.reuters.com/article/2012/09/21/uk-myanmar-thailand-dawei-idUSLNE88K00R20120921
53. Joseph Allchin, "Burma Lobbies for More Thai Investment," *Democratic Voice of Burma*,13 July 2010. Available: http://www.dvb.no/news/burma-lobbies-for-more-thai-investment/10710
54. "Thailand sees Big Potential for Myanmar," *The Financial Express*, 14 February 2012. Available: http://www.thefinancialexpress-bd.com/more.php?news_id=98536&date=2012-02-14.
55. Gwen Robinson, "Thailand's PTT to Invest $3bn in Myanmar," *Financial Express*, 17 July 2012. Available: http://www.ft.com/cms/s/0/14074a42-d013-11e1-bcaa-00144feabdc0.html#axzz2OZMeWVyc
56. "South Korea wants more Investments in Burma," *Mizzima*, 15 March 2012. Available: http://www.mizzima.com/business/6767-south-korea-wants-more-investments-in-burma.html
57. "Myanmar Gets Record Investment After Years of Isolation: Energy," *Bloomberg*, 17 September 2012. Available: http://www.bloomberg.com/news/2012-09-16/myanmar-gets-record-investment-after-years-of-isolation-energy.html
58. "PepsiCo Announces Myanmar Distribution Agreement with Diamond Star," PepsiCo, 09 August 2012. Available: http://www.pepsico.com/pressrelease/pepsico-announces-myanmar-distribution-agreement-with-diamond-star08092012.html
59. Narayan Lakshman, "India Should tell Myanmar to Change Course: U.S. ," *The Hindu*, July 24, 2010. Available: http://www.thehindu.com/news/international/article531961.ece

9
Recent Trends and Developments on Connectivity between India and Myanmar: A Borderland Perspective

K. Yhome

Myanmar has witnessed dramatic developments in the recent past as the country moves towards a more open political system and re-engages with the international community after long years of isolation. These developments have been taking place alongside rapidly changing strategic and economic dynamics in the region. Prime Minister Manmohan Singh's visit to Myanmar in May 2012 has firmed up relations with its eastern neighbour at a time when other countries are positioning themselves to make the most of 'New Myanmar'. As Myanmar re-engages the international community, Delhi recognizes that it needs to strengthen its ties with Myanmar to promote and protect its strategic interests in the East. Delhi's role in the process of change now will determine what influence it will have in that country in future.

Within this context, a renewed focus has been given on regional connectivity following a few major high-level official visits. During Prime Minister Manmohan Singh's visit to Myanmar, Delhi and Nay Pyi Taw agreed to make the India-Myanmar-Thailand trilateral highway project "a reality" by 2016.[1] When the Thai Prime Minister, Yingluck Shinawatra visited India in January 2012, the joint statement issued talked about "an economic corridor linking India with Thailand and Southeast Asia."[2] Earlier, Myanmar's President Thein Sein visited India in October 2011 during which the two countries reemphasized the importance of connectivity.[3] In the backdrop of these developments, this chapter examines how India plans to build linkages with Myanmar and beyond, and analyse the motivations of this renewed focus.

Even as the two nations share rich cultural and historical linkages, the current presence of each in the popular imagination of the other is dismally low and they have remained distant neighbours. After witnessing a warm relationship soon after Independence, bilateral relationship stagnated as the leadership in Myanmar looked inward in its policy orientation and India remained pre-occupied with its western border. In the past decade or so, India's Myanmar policy has been driven largely by its security, energy and strategic considerations.[4] The limited engagement has, however, laid the ground for the two neighbours to take their relationship to a higher level. This is in spite of the fact that the political stalemate in Myanmar, between the military regime and pro-democracy movement, coupled with New Delhi's own sluggish policy implementation has impeded the growth of the relationship.

The overall India-Myanmar bilateral relations have been on the upswing in the recent years.[5] Political relations have improved, economic and security ties have been strengthened and there is no lack of policies and initiatives in strengthening ties and boosting cooperation between the two countries. The relationship has also demonstrated a degree of maturity in the past decade. While political and security ties have shown progress, economic relations remain much below its potential. Despite the recent interest shown by Indian private companies in Myanmar, the overall trade and investment figures remain low. As of 2011-12, India's approved investment in Myanmar was US$ 273 million and the total bilateral trade was US$ 1.87 billion, out of which border trade accounted an estimated US$ 15.41 million.[6] It may be noted that the figure excludes the huge unaccounted informal trade at the border.

Prime Minister Manmohan Singh's visit to Myanmar was an effort to provide the push in the bilateral relationship as Myanmar tries to rebalance its external engagements. Delhi has used the visit to reaffirm its willingness to strengthen the relationship with its eastern neighbour, and with the hope that Myanmar becomes the bridge and acts as a gateway in reaching the East. Prime Minister Manmohan Singh's visit has sent a strong message to Myanmar that Delhi attaches importance to developments in its strategically important eastern neighbour. The current changes and the future direction Myanmar will take will have immense implications for India. The warming of relations between Nay Pyi Taw and Washington and other major powers are in India's long-term interest as this adds to the efforts of counter-balancing the increasing Chinese presence in Myanmar. Delhi would not want to see China having an overwhelming influence in a country that is strategically important for India. The entry of other players gives Myanmar more strategic options and, for India, a strong Myanmar that maintains a neutral policy towards major powers is in its interest.

Prime Minister Manmohan Singh's visit has further deepened ties and built the foundation for a strategic relationship that binds the two with elements of shared values that ensures mutual benefits and regional stability. The two countries agreed on a wide-range of areas for cooperation that included the development of border areas, enhancing connectivity, strengthening trade ties, promoting people-to-people contacts, and extending assistance for capacity-building. That Myanmar is moving towards a democratic form of government is in tandem with India's own democratic values. More importantly, sharing India's parliamentary and democratic experiences with Myanmar's political parties could go a long way in strengthening Myanmar's nascent democracy. The visit has charted out a long-term plan for enduring cooperation and mutual benefits, thereby laying the ground for strengthening and broad-basing engagement between the two neighbours.

Geographical and Development Imperatives

Connectivity and development cooperation between India and Myanmar were reemphasized during Manmohan Singh's visit to Myanmar, a clear indication of Delhi's renewed interest in geography and development. The emerging approach is recognizable in the Joint

Statement issued during the Prime Minister's Myanmar visit.[7] The renewed approach is an effort to correct the lopsidedness in the policy thereby giving geographical and development factors their due importance in India's engagement with Myanmar. This is reflected in Delhi's broadening of its engagement with Myanmar to include the social and development sectors. Among the Southeast Asian countries, Myanmar is the only country that shares a land boundary with India and both India and Myanmar share maritime boundaries in the Bay of Bengal. In fact, the growing bilateral and regional connectivity projects are recognition of this fact.

There have been significant transformations in borderlands in the past two decades or so. In the context of the economic rise of India and East Asia, particularly, China and Southeast Asian countries, India's Northeast has found itself at "a crossroads."[8] The force of economic integration has been quietly, but surely integrating the region with economies of the neighbouring countries having the potential of changing the landscape of the region.[9] As these economies grow and integrate further, India's Northeast will find itself embedded in the larger commercial interests of the external players, for whom peace and stability are paramount for economic activities. While the overall economic development remains far from desired, the relative peace in the Northeast region over the past years has also led to the development of some places and growth of consumer culture in the region. The political economy of the region has also been undergoing dramatic changes. While military means and formal political negotiations have failed to bring about peace in the Northeast region, the question is: Can the structure of armed conflicts remain unaffected in future in the rapidly changing economic dynamics?"

The paradigm shift in the way nation-states look at their borders from "frontiers" to "land bridges" or "gateways" has been a major motivation of this change. In the past few years, there has been a relook at the whole borderland discourse and the dominant theme that has emerged is the rethinking in seeing borderlands from a discourse dominated largely by the "security" paradigm to seeing as being economic "gateways". The end of the Cold War in the late 1980s saw new realignments of relations driven less by ideological factors, but more by economic interests. And in the era of globalization, "connectivity" has become the buzzword. The regaining of importance of borderlands in regional diplomacy, not only from the security and strategic perspectives, but also from economic and connectivity dimensions are based largely on the notion that political boundaries will gradually become "irrelevant" in the era of globalization. The renewed interests of the governments on borderlands have prompted the need to view the borderlands from geo-economic perspective. India's Northeast is today seen as a "land bridge" linking India with Myanmar and beyond and from being a "landlocked" to a "land-linked" region.[10]

India and Myanmar share some of the most "volatile frontiers" in Asia.[11] The two neighbours have several common social, economic and security issues along their shared border. Delhi and Nay Pyi Taw are aware that in dealing with these issues, they need each others' help. Working out a common strategy for development of their border regions will serve well in resolving some of the long-standing ethnic unrest on both sides of the border, as well as other border-related security issues. Increased connectivity to boost economic activities in the border regions will be central to this effort. During Manmohan Singh's visit, the two countries have, for the first time, signed Memorandum of Understandings (MoUs) to cooperate in border area development. India-Myanmar border area development initiatives are also the acknowledgment of the geographical compulsions.

The MoU related to border development are the MoU on the India-Myanmar Border Area Development and the MoU on establishing of Border Haats across the border between Myanmar and India. The initiatives are aimed at cooperating in the socio-economic development of the border areas by focusing on projects, such as education, health, and agriculture and other basic infrastructure, like roads and bridges. The need to cooperate in these areas was a result of the recognition that security issues cannot be resolved through military means alone. There was a need for an approach that encompasses the overall development of the bordering areas. Hence, linking development with security is a major step forward in dealing with border areas. This initiative also underscores the importance of the role of local civilians, thus, giving them a stake in the improvement of the bilateral relationship between the two neighbours. While, the "special focus" on the border areas is significant, the reality is that there are a number of ethnic armed groups that are still active on both sides of the border. It is, therefore, equally important that both New Delhi and Nay Pyi Taw continue their efforts to find lasting political settlements with the insurgent groups. Any effort to develop the border areas and to achieve the goals set by the two would need a peaceful and stable border region.

For both Delhi and Nay Pyi Taw, economic development that respects local sensitivities and benefits the local population of India's Northeast and Myanmar's Northwestern region are the answers to resolve the decades-old armed violence that has long characterized the two regions. Ethnic communities along the India-Myanmar border have long been seen as a security problem and the recent efforts to make them stakeholders in the bilateral relationship have been to evolve a new paradigm in bilateral relationship between India and Myanmar. The MoU signed during the Prime Minister's visit to operationalize the US$ 500-million line of credit announced during President Thein Sein's visit to India in October 2011 would increase India's role in the development of Myanmar. Under the MoU, India will extend to Myanmar the concessional credit line that will be utilized in infrastructure development projects, including in agriculture, irrigation, rail transport and power. The credit line is in addition to nearly US$ 300 million extended earlier for several infrastructural projects.[12]

The Kaladan Multi-Modal Transit Transport Facility

One of the most important physical connectivity projects is the Kaladan project agreed between the two countries on 2 April 2008, after almost a decade of negotiation. The link has been planned through an inland waterway connecting the port of Sittwe and Setpyitpyin (Kalewa) along the Kaladan (or Kolodyne) River known as Chhimtuipui River in Mizoram and a highway linking Kaletwa to the India-Myanmar border in the state of Mizoram (see Figure 9.1

below). The key components of the project include the construction of a port/Inland Water Transport (IWT) terminal and related infrastructure facilities at the port of Sittwe in Myanmar for trans-shipment to inland vessels and vice versa, including the development of the navigation channels; dredging of the 225 km Kaladan waterway from Sittwe to Paletwa; construction of a highway from Kalewa to India-Myanmar border and maintenance and management of these facilities.[13]

Figure 9.1: The Kaladan Project linking Kolkata with India's Northeast through Sittwe in Myanmar

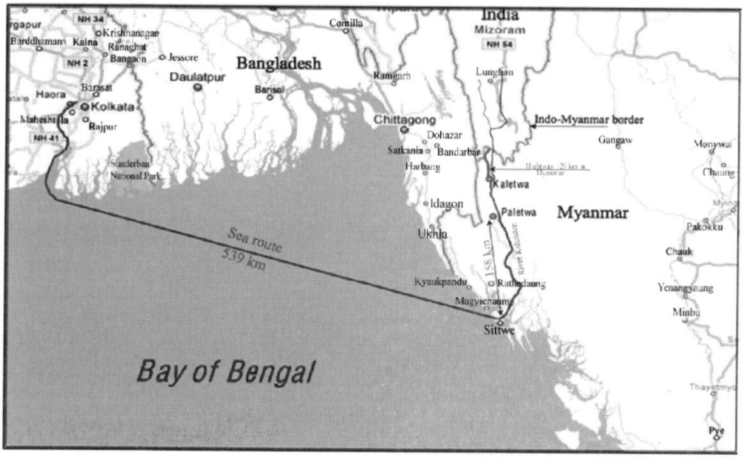

Source: Arakan Rivers Network http://www.arakanrivers.net/?page_id=135

The idea of connecting the Northeast with the rest of the country through inland waterway is not new. During the colonial period, water transport was the main route for trade between the Northeast and other provinces and steamer service on the Brahmaputra river between Kolkata and Guwahati was introduced as early as 1847.[14] The technical feasibility study for IWT on river Kaladan and highway along the river Kaladan from Sittwe to India-Myanmar border (Mizoram) was conducted by RITES Ltd. (under the Ministry of Railways) during 1999-2000 and its report was submitted to the Ministry of External Affairs (MEA), in March 2001.[15] In July 2001, the two countries agreed to carry out the first phase of the project and a Detailed Project Report (DPR) prepared by RITES was submitted in 2003 at a total project cost of US$ 68.24 million as on 2003 for the Sittwe port and the Kaladan waterway, and US$ 49.14 for the construction of a road from Kalewa to India-Myanmar border, to be funded by the Government of India and handover the project to the Government of Myanmar on completion.[16]

In March 2008, the Government of India sanctioned Rs. 535.91 crores for the construction of the road.[17] The Inland Waterways Authority of India (IWAI) was appointed in March 2009 by the MEA as the project development consultant that submitted a revised DPR for the port and IWT components of the project in September 2009. On 14 May 2010, the MEA signed a contract with Mumbai-based Essar Projects (India) Ltd. as the main contractor for the port and IWT works at a contract price of Rs 342 crores to be completed by June 2013.[18] The contract involves the construction of two jetties at Sittwe and Paletwa in Myanmar, dredging and construction of cargo barges to facilitate cargo movement along the river Kaladan. The construction of the port and IWT works started in December 2010 with equipments and materials from India arriving at the construction site.[19] The other component of the multimodal transit transport project is the 62 km road from the river terminal to the Indo-Myanmar border.[20] A land customs station is being proposed at Zorinpui in the southern tip of Mizoram to facilitate the trade between the two countries.[21]

India's Northeast is comprised of eight states (Assam, Arunachal Pradesh, Nagaland, Manipur, Mizoram, Meghalaya, Tripura and Sikkim) surrounded by five countries with China to the north, Nepal and Bhutan to the northwest, Myanmar to the east and Bangladesh to the south. The region is connected to the rest of the country through a narrow stretch of land (21-40 km in width) between Nepal and Bangladesh known as the Siliguri corridor or the "Chicken's Neck". The need for an alternate route to connect the Northeast has stemmed for both economic and strategic reasons. Given the landlocked nature of the region, the idea of the Kaladan project is not only to link the region to the Bay of Bengal area for access to the sea, but also to link the Northeast region with the rest of the country.

The Kaladan project has been designed to establish an ocean route connecting main economic centres of India to the Northeast region through Myanmar.

One of the objectives of the Kaladan project is to get around the problem of Bangladesh's intransigence in allowing transit rights through its territory to the Northeast region. It also aimed at easing pressure on the strategically important Siliguri corridor, thus providing a route for alternate access to the Northeast region. Another aim of the project is to add to the efforts of development in the Northeast region in addressing the vicious cycle of underdevelopment, which is seen as a source of insurgency in the region. For several decades, the "geographical isolation" of the region has been viewed as one of the key development constraints.[22] This notion of the region may soon change.[23] The development of the Kaladan project will link the region to the sea, which will increase economic activities and generate jobs in the region. While the development of Kaladan project will ease the movement of goods from the rest of the country to the Northeast region, it will also help Myanmar to develop its infrastructure and port facilities, which will accelerate development in the country.

There is also a paradigm shift in Delhi's approach towards the Northeast region. For decades, the region was seen only through the prism of security. This is changing. There is a growing recognition of the notion that economic integration of the Northeast region with the neighbouring countries is needed for its development.[24] This notion in turn has been influenced by two factors. First, the security issues in the Northeast region cannot be resolved by military means alone and secondly, "frontiers" are increasingly seen as "gateways". The rapid economic growth in Southeast and East Asia has made Myanmar the bridge between India and the East Asian economies and the Northeast region as the bridgehead.[25]

The India-Myanmar-Thailand Trilateral Highway Project

Given its central geographical location at a crossroads, in regional and sub-regional connectivity between India, Southeast and East Asia,

Myanmar has naturally become the "land-bridge". One such project is the India-Myanmar-Thailand Trilateral Highway (IMTTH), "a cross-border transportation network financed by the governments of three countries and developed by the public sector." The 1360 km highway would link Moreh in India to Mae Sot in Thailand through Bagan in Myanmar. The alignment of the highway falls within the Asian Highways 1 and 2, being pursued by United Nations Economic and Social Commission for Asia and the Pacific (UNESCAP).[26] The agreed route of the IMTTH is identified as follows: Moreh (India)-Tamu-Kalewa-Chaungma-Yinmabin-Pale-Kyadat-Lingadow-Pakokku-Bagan-Kyaukpadaung-Meiktilabypass-Taungoo-Oktwin-Payagyi-Theinzayat-Thaton-Hypaan-Kawkareik-Myawaddy-Mae Sot (Thailand).[27] The trilateral highway is an initiative of the Mekong-Ganga Cooperation Initiative (MGC), a sub-regional cooperation scheme between India and five riparian countries of the Mekong River, namely, Cambodia, Lao PDR, Myanmar, Thailand, and Vietnam.

Figure 9.2: The India-Myanmar-Thailand Trilateral Highway Project

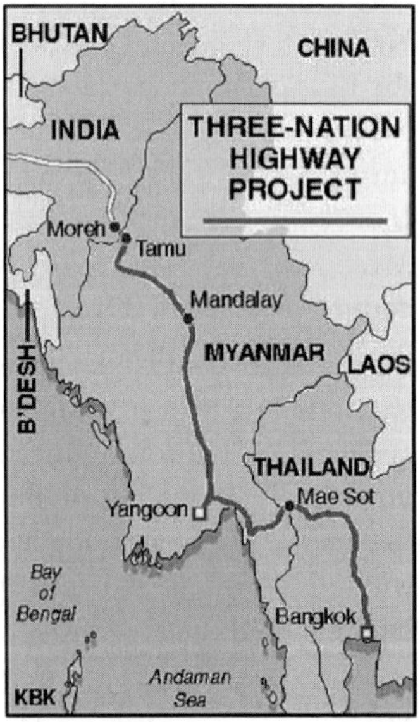

Source: The Tribune, 24 December, 2003. Available at http://www.tribuneindia.com/2003/20031224/biz.htm#5

The Trilateral Highway is divided into three phases: Phase-I includes Moreh (India)-Tamu-Kalewa-Chaungma-Yinmabin-Pale-Kyadat-Lingadow-Pakokku-Bagan-Kyaukpadaung-Meiktilabypass-Taungoo-Oktwin-Payagyi-Theinzayat sector; Phase-II comprises Thaton-Hypaan-Kawkareik sector; and Phase-III includes Myawaddy-Mae Sot (Thailand) sector of the project. Since the MGC was formally launched on 10 November 2000 in the Laotian capital of Vientiane, the key areas of cooperation have been tourism, culture, education, and transport and communication.[28] The Vientiane Declaration adopted in the first MGC Ministerial Meeting committed itself to strengthen connectivity among the member-countries. Among other things, it talked about developing transport networks, particularly, the 'East-West Corridor' and the 'Trans-Asian Highways' under the rubric of transport and communication. The first India-Myanmar-Thailand Ministerial Meeting on Transport Linkages was held on 5-6 April 2002 in Myanmar. In the third Ministerial Meeting of the MGC countries held in Phnom Penh on 20 June 2003, the ministers reaffirmed their support to the Trilateral Highway project. In a foreign ministers' meeting in Delhi in December 2003, the three countries agreed to commence the construction of the Phase-I of the Highway in early 2004, but it actually began in 2005, at an estimated cost of US$ 700 million -US$ 252 million in the first Phase, US$ 154 million in the second phase and US$ 284 million in the third Phase.[29]

India has been involved in infrastructure development to improve connectivity between India and Myanmar. A 160-km long Tamu-Kalemyo-Kalewa in Myanmar's Sagaing Region was constructed by the Border Road Organization (BRO) of India at a cost of Rs. 1.20 billion (about US$ 27.28 million) and inaugurated in February 2001 and named as India-Myanmar Friendship Road. The government of India had maintained the road till 2009 when it was handed over to Myanmar. The last 28 km stretch from Kyigone to Kalewa was completed in April 2012.[30]

The Trilateral Highway work was stalled since 2006, mainly due to political reasons in Myanmar. Lack of essential institutional support and government commitments are seen as other reasons for slowing down of development of the trilateral highway. It has been argued that deeper regional cooperation among the three countries (perhaps within BIMSTEC) would help in the development of the trilateral highway.[31]

Giving a major boost to the trilateral highway, during his visit to Myanmar Prime Minister Manmohan Singh announced that India will repair and upgrade 71 bridges on the Tamu-Kalewa Friendship Road and the two countries agreed to make the trilateral highway a reality by 2016. Earlier, the Joint Task Force on Trilateral Highway among India, Myanmar and Thailand was revived. Delhi also committed to undertake the up-gradation of the Kalewa-Yargyi road segment to highway standard and Myanmar agreed to upgrade the Yargyi-Monywa stretch to highway standard.

India's objectives to promote its linkages with the ASEAN region are multidimensional. Since its adoption of the "Look East" policy in the early 1990s, the policy has evolved from economic to acquire strategic elements.[32] The trilateral highway project is an important component of India's endeavour to reach out to ASEAN. Delhi's efforts have received applause from the Southeast Asian countries. For instance, the trilateral highway has been supported by the ASEAN grouping: "We also highly appreciated India's strong commitment to support the implementation of the Master Plan on ASEAN Connectivity (MPAC)…. We reiterated our strategic objective in greater physical connectivity, including land and sea connectivity. These include the India-Myanmar-Thailand Highway, its extension to Laos and Cambodia and the development of a new highway also linking Vietnam."[33]

This reciprocal interest between India and ASEAN is a result of the fast growing economic ties. India is today the seventh largest trading partner of ASEAN and the sixth largest investor in ASEAN with an increase of 40.8 per cent in the foreign direct investment from India to ASEAN in 2009. In fact, India-ASEAN trade has increased by 30 per cent in 2010-2011 and has crossed the US$ 50 billion. With US$ 80 billion trade in 2011-2012, India and ASEAN have set a bilateral trade target of US$ 100 billion by 2015 to be achieved.[34]

Apart from economic interest, Delhi's engagement with Southeast Asia has also been to strengthen its cultural linkages in the region with the hope to promote and increase its image and influence in the region. India had civilizational linkages with Southeast Asia and through cultural diplomacy, New Delhi wants to revive those old cultural ties. This is evident from various sub-regional initiatives between India and the Southeast Asian countries. Both MGC and the BIMSTEC have focused on people-to-people contact, tourism, culture, and education. Connectivity is seen as one of the key to strengthen the areas identified for cooperation. It is with this aim that enhanced transport and communication is being promoted by the member-countries. India and Thailand have been cooperating closely on improving regional connectivity not only through the trilateral highway, but also with other initiatives, such as the Asian Highway Network (under UNESCAP) and BIMSTEC Transport Infrastructure and Logistics Study (BTILS) under the BIMSTEC framework.[35]

The other dimension of India's interest for closer integration with Southeast Asian countries is strategic in nature. The rise of China and its growing presence in the Southeast Asia is a source of concern for New Delhi. In the larger regional geostrategic environment of Asia, the Southeast Asian countries have played an important role because of its central location and as a key player in the evolving security and economic architecture in the region. Given the importance of ASEAN in the region, Delhi understands that it cannot afford to remain a silent spectator in the evolving regional geostrategic environment. The Southeast Asian region has vital maritime trade routes including the Malacca Strait and the South China Sea, where India's dependence is growing over the years as its seaborne trade increases with East Asia. Through closer coordination in bilateral and multilateral frameworks, India seeks to further integrate itself with ASEAN, with the hope that it will limit China's influence in the region. China's economic integration with the Southeast Asian countries, particularly, the Mekong region have been attributed to the large regional connectivity networks that China has built in the past two decades. India is a latecomer in connecting itself with Southeast Asia.

The Chennai-Dawei Corridor

In recent years, particularly, since Myanmar began to open up, an important focus has been on how Myanmar can become a "new gateway" connecting India with Southeast Asia.[36] A maritime route that links India's southern city of Chennai (formerly Madras) in the State of Tamil Nadu and Myanmar's southern coastal town of Dawei

Figure 9.3: The Dawei Project and the Chennai-Dawei Corridor

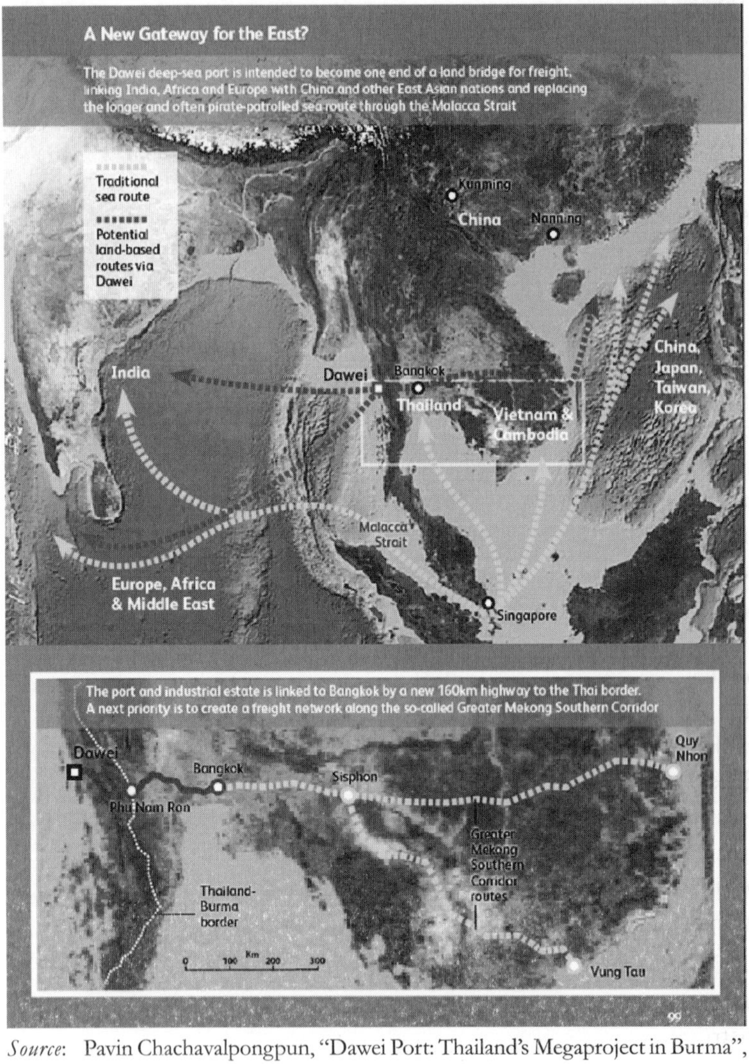

Source: Pavin Chachavalpongpun, "Dawei Port: Thailand's Megaproject in Burma", *Global Asia*, December, 2011. Available at http://www.globalasia.org/V6N4_Winter_2011/Pavin_Chachavalpongpun.html?PHPSESSID=27e2e5f1eea77f9e245c911358886d55

in the Tenasserim State has been dubbed as the Chennai-Dawei Corridor. The interest on this corridor among regional governments has gained currency in the context of the Dawei Project. In early 2008, Myanmar and Thailand agreed to develop a deep sea port in Dawei and connect it through a road link to Bangkok. Under the Framework Agreement signed between Thai construction firm, Italian-Thai Development Public Company Limited (ITD) and Myanma Port Authority, the ITD was awarded 75-year concession to build and operate the port and industrial estate. The project includes the development of the Dawei deep seaport, industrial estate, transborder corridor, highways and railroad links to Thailand. The entire project is estimated at more than US$ 58 billion.[37] The idea of developing a deep sea port in Dawei was originally discussed years ago by Thailand as an alternative route to the Straits of Malacca.[38]

Though Thailand is the key player in the Dawei project, India's interest in the development of the port has gone through different phases. Much before Thailand and Myanmar agreed to develop the Dawei project, in 2004, Delhi had offered to conduct a feasibility study on Dawei deep sea port and road linkage between the port and Kanchanburi in Thailand.[39] However, for inexplicable reasons, Delhi stayed out of the project. It is only recently that Delhi is again showing interest in the project. During the visit of the Thai Prime Minister Yingluck Shinawatra to India in January 2012, she invited India to help in the construction of the Dawei deep sea port. In response to which, Prime Minister Manmohan Singh offered support.[40] Addressing the leaders of Indian industry in Delhi, Thai Prime Minister Shinawatra said: "My government has decided to invest in transport and connect with our neighbours. We could set up a maritime linkage with Chennai and Dawei seaport in Myanmar along with road connectivity."[41]

Since then, Delhi has taken every opportunity to discuss the Dawei port project with Thailand and Myanmar. If the Dawei port is constructed, it will take only two days for a product to be transported from Chennai to Dawei, and another day from Dawei to Bangkok. During Myanmar's Foreign Minister, Wunna Maung Lwin's visit to Delhi in January 2012, he discussed the Trilateral Highway and Dawei project with Indian External Affairs Minister S.M. Krishna.[42] In August 2012, during the India-Thailand Foreign Office Consultations meeting in Bangkok, officials of both countries again re-emphasised the importance of connectivity and discussed the implementation of the Trilateral Highway and the Dawei port project.[43]

In the past, Chennai and other coastal cities had flourishing maritime linkages with Myanmar, particularly Yangon (formerly Rangoon). Until the 1990s, ferry services operated between Chennai and Yangon. During the visit of President Thein Sein to India in October 2011, the two countries agreed to restart ferry services between the two countries, and as a first step have decided to start ferry services on Kolkata-Yangon and Chennai-Yangon routes.[44] Following these developments, shipping companies have shown interest in linking Indian ports with Myanmar. On 31 July 2012, Gati Ship Pvt. Ltd, a subsidiary of the Hyderabad-based express distribution company of Gati Ltd, has announced a dedicated shipping route service connecting Chennai-Yangon-Chennai with the aim to "help businesses maximize trade potential" between India and Myanmar.[45]

Even as the corridor will provide an alternative route to Southeast Asia, the commercial and strategic advantages also attract Delhi to be part of the project. Once the corridor is developed, "shipping time between Thailand and India could be cut in half."[46] Currently, transporting goods from India to Thailand takes six days, as the route ships through the Straits of Malacca. India enjoys good relations with Southeast Asian countries, particularly those strategically important—Singapore, Malaysia, and Indonesia that sits across the Strait. However, in the recent years, the issue of piracy in the Straits has been a source of concern[47] and in the event of conflict, the narrow Strait is vulnerable to be used as a choke-point. In the increasing maritime rivalry among major powers, the Chennai-Dawei corridor could provide a strategic outlet to India to reach Southeast Asia and beyond.

Conclusion

The future of borderlands remains uncertain. While the prospects of borderlands becoming Asia's "new crosswords" of prosperity have been talked about,[48] equally, they could become new battlegrounds of great power rivalry.[49] However, the growing linkages would mean that Border States will increasingly become key stakeholders in regional diplomacy. Their interests, fears and expectations together with policies and stability of the border regions will play a critical role in achieving the desired goals that connectivity projects offers. Hence, there is a need to reconsider the traditional notions on the conduct of regional diplomacy, and debate on new ideas for mutual benefits by involving all key stakeholders to play a role in foreign policy making.

Involving the provincial governments of the border regions in regional diplomacy—in sub-regional groupings, such as the BIMSTEC and the Mekong-Ganga Cooperation may inject new dynamism in transforming these sub-regional groupings. In the context of the ongoing changes taking place in Myanmar, both India and Myanmar have an opportunity to revitalize their approaches towards their borderlands. With Southeast Asian countries showing greater interest in Northeast India, the likelihood of the projects seeing the light of the day is high.

As immediate neighbours, sharing long land and maritime boundaries, India and Myanmar have little choice, but to engage with each other closely. Such engagements, particularly after a long span of time needs understanding of each other's political and strategic concerns, and help in the development of social and economic interest of the other. Prime Minister Manmohan Singh's visit laid the foundation for an enduring relationship between India and Myanmar. However, on the connectivity projects, there are voices of opposition against the projects, on the ground that these projects would have adverse environmental and social implications.[50] In fact, in March 2012, the Myanmar government agreed to conduct environment and social impact assessment to minimize negative effect of the Kaladan project on local population.[51]

While there is growing recognition among various governments and policy-makers about the need to link border regions, there are still not many, who talk about the role of local provincial governments in regional diplomacy. "Constituent Diplomacy"[52] is not new in international diplomacy parlance, as it has been in existence both as a concept and in practice in other parts of the world. The concept has been defined as "the participation of regional and local governments in foreign policy making and international affairs".[53] According to the Constituent Diplomacy Paradigm, the provincial governments have a prominent role in the making of foreign economic policy. In the context of the changing nature of borderlands, India and Myanmar may have to relook at the way they treat their borderlands. There is a need to expand the civilian space over military and the legal space over illegal. All key stakeholders should play an active role in the process of foreign policy making, as they are directly affected, thus, giving them a stake in regional diplomacy.

Delhi's reemphasis on geography and development in its relations with Myanmar meets the needs of the changing dynamics of the border areas. The success of the approach will depend on how effectively the current projects are implemented and how innovatively new projects are formulated in line with that approach. The Kaladan Project was initially expected to be completed in 2012, but the project will not become a reality in the next few years. Again, while there are several other linkages that can be developed between the two countries, it may be prudent to first focus on the completion of the ongoing projects. Developmental activities in the border areas and the connectivity projects would inevitably increase the role of the border states in the bilateral relations between the two neighbours.

REFERENCES

1. See "Joint Statement on the occasion of the visit of Prime Minister of India Dr. Manmohan Singh to Myanmar", 28 May, 2012. Available at http://pmindia.nic.in/press-details.php?nodeid=1439.
2. See "Joint Statement by India and Thailand on the State Visit of Prime Minister of Thailand Yingluck Shinawatra to India", 25 January, 2012. Available at http://pmindia.nic.in/press-details.php?nodeid=1351
3. See "Joint Statement on the occasion of the State Visit of the President of the Republic of the Union of Myanmar to India", 14 October, 2011. Available at http://mea.gov.in/incoming-visit-detail.htm?5326/Joint+Statement+on+the+occasion+of+the+State+Visit+of+the+President+of+the+Republic+of+the+Union+of+Myanmar+to+India

4. For recent assessments on India-Myanmar relations see Renaud Egreteau, "A passage to Burma? India, development, and democratization in Myanmar", *Contemporary Politics*, Vol. 17, No. 4, December 2011, pp. 467-486; C. Raja Mohan, "Embracing Myanmar: India's foreign policy realism", *RSIS Commentary* No. 86/201, 2010; Renaud Egreteau, "India and China vying for influence in Burma: a new assessment" *India Review*, 7 (1), 2008, pp. 38-72; Renaud Egreteau, "India's ambitions in Burma: more frustration than success?", *Asian Survey*, 48 (6), 2008, pp. 936-957; Marie Lall, "India-Myanmar relations: geopolitics and energy in light of the new power of balance in Asia", ISAS Working Paper No. 29, 2 January, 2008; and K. Yhome, "India-Myanmar Relations (1998-2008): A Decade of Redefining Bilateral Ties," *Occasional Paper* 10 (New Delhi: Observer Research Foundation, January 2008); Marie Lall, "Indo-Myanmar relations in the era of pipeline diplomacy", *Contemporary Southeast Asia*, 28 (3), 2006, pp. 424-446.
5. For two contradictory views on India-Myanmar relations in the past decade see Renaud Egreteau, "India's ambitions in Burma: more frustration than success?", *Asian Survey*, 48 (6), 2008, pp. 936-957 and K. Yhome, "India-Myanmar Relations (1998-2008): A Decade of Redefining Bilateral Ties," *Occasional Paper* 10 (New Delhi: Observer Research Foundation, January 2008).
6. See official website of the Embassy of India, Yangon, Myanmar. Available at http://www.indiaembassy.net.mm/index.php?option=com_content&view=article&id=165&Itemid=62&lang=en
7. See "Joint Statement on the occasion of the visit of Prime Minister of India Dr. Manmohan Singh to Myanmar", 28 May, 2012. Available at http://pmindia.nic.in/press-details.php?nodeid=1439
8. See Thant Myint-U, *"Where China Meets India: Burma and the New Crossroads of Asia*", (New York: Farrar, Straus and Girous: 2011).
9. For recent analyses on India's Northeast see Subir Bhaumik, *Troubled Periphery: Crisis of India's North East* (New Delhi: Sage Publications, 2009); Sanjib Baruah, *Beyond Counterinsurgency: Breaking the Impasse in Northeast India* (New Delhi: Oxford University Press, 2009).
10. See the keynote address by Shashi Tharoor, Minister of State for External Affairs, in the International Conference on "From Land Locked to Land Linked: North East India in BIMSTEC", on April 9, 2010, North Eastern Hills University, Shillong. Available at http://www.jneis.com/?p=159
11. See Bertil Linter, *Great Game East: India, China and the Struggle for Asia's Most Volatile Frontier*, (New Delhi: HarperCollins, 2012).
12. See *The Times of India*, 15 October, 2011 and *The Tribune*, 15 October, 2011.
13. See full text of the "Framework Agreement between the Government of the Republic of India and the Government of the Union of Myanmar for the Construction and Operation of a Multi-Modal Transit Transport Facility on the Kaladan River Connecting the Sittwe Port in Myanmar with the State of

Mizoram", found at the official website of the Inland Waterways Authority of India, Ministry of Shipping, Government of India. Available at http://iwai.gov.in/nit/Frameworkagreement.pdf (accessed on 1 July, 2012). Also see Ministry of Development of North Eastern Region (DONER), Government of India at http://www.mdoner.gov.in/writereaddata/sublink2images/KaladanMultiModal2172726384.htm (accessed on 12 June, 2012).

14. See "Perspectives of Inland Water Transport: Development of the Northeast", Inland Waterways Authority of India, Background Paper No. 7, January 2007. p. 23. Available at http://mdoner.gov.in/writereaddata/sublink3images/77330284159.pdf
15. Official website of the Inland Waterways Authority of India, Ministry of Shipping, Government of India, http://iwai.gov.in/misc/portiwt.pdf (accessed on 12 July, 2012)
16. See "Framework Agreement between the Government of the Republic of India and The Government of the Union of Myanmar for the Construction and Operation of a Multi-Modal Transit Transport Facility on the Kaladan River Connecting the Sittwe Port in Myanmar with the State of Mizoram", found at the official website of the Inland Waterways Authority of India, Ministry of Shipping, Government of India. Available at http://iwai.gov.in/nit/Frameworkagreement.pdf (accessed on 1 July, 2012). Also see Appendex II, *Report of the Task Force on Connectivity and Promotion of Trade and Investments in NE States",* Planning Commission, Government of India, October 2006.
17. *Livemint*, 27 March, 2008. Available at http://www.livemint.com/Politics/PIxAxYZcAcPoTIhZ2Oa4QL/Govt-okays-Rs535-cr-Myanmar-project-to-help-North-East.html
18. See official website of the Essar Group. Available at http://www.essar.com/article.aspx?cont_id=ywBmcC5QmHU (accessed on 1 July, 2012)
19. Official website of the Inland Waterways Authority of India, Ministry of Shipping, Government of India, http://iwai.gov.in/misc/KALADANPROJECTSTATUSJAN11040111.pdf (accessed on 12 July, 2012)
20. "Executive Summary of Detailed Project Report for a Highway from Setpyitpyin (Kaletwa) to India-Myanmar Border in Myanmar", Inland Waterway Authorty of India. Available at http://iwai.gov.in/misc/highway.pdf
21. In April 2012 Myanmar's Ambassador to India visited the site to inspect the proposed station in Mizoram.
22. Laldinkima Sailo, "Northeast India: Trade and Developemnt Prospects", *ISAS Insights*, No. 171, 25 June 2012, Institute of South Asian Studies, Singapore.
23. As Thant Myint-U argues in his book: "What had been remote is now closer to the new centre." See Thant Myint-U, *"Where China Meets India: Burma and the New Crossroads of Asia"*, (New York: Farrar, Straus and Girous: 2011, p. 107).
24. See Jiaram Ramesh, "Northeast India in a new Asia", in *Seminar* # 550, June

2005. Available at http://www.india-seminar.com/2005/550/550%20jairam%20ramesh.htm

25. Lal Pudaite, "Chapter 6—Mizoram", in Mayumi Murayama, Kyoko Inoue, Sanjoy Hazarika (eds.), Sub-Regional Relations in the Eastern South Asia: With Special Focus on India's North Eastern Region, Joint Research Programme Series, No. 133, Institute of Developing Economies, Japan External Trade Organization, February 2005 (http://www.ide.go.jp/English/Publish/Download/Jrp/pdf/133_8.pdf). Accessed on 24 July, 2012.
26. *Asian Highway Handbook*, Economic and Social Commission for Asia and the Pacific, United Nations, New York, 2003. See Country pages of India. Myanmar and Thailand.
27. Prabir De, "ASEAN-India Connectivity: An Indian Perspective", in Fukunari Kimura and So Umezaki (eds.), *ASEAN-India Connectivity: The Comprehensive Asia Development Plan, Phase II*, ERIA Research Project Report 2010-7. March 2011, p. 138. Available at http://www.eria.org/publications/research_project_reports/images/pdf/y2010/no7/3_India.pdf
28. See *Annual Report 2000-2001*, Ministry of External Affairs, Government of India. Available at http://mea.gov.in/meaxpsite/annualreport/ar20002001.pdf (accessed on 27 July 2012)
29. *The Tribune*, 24 December, 2003.
30. *Indo Asian News Service* (IANS) 22 June, 2011. Found at http://in.finance.yahoo.com/news/India-Myanmar-ink-pact-border-ians-180882017.html (accessed on 12 July, 2012).
31. Prabir De, Muthi Samudram, and Sanjeev Moholkar, "Trends in National and Regional Investors Financing Crossborder Infrastructure Projects in Asia", *ADBI Working Paper Series,* No. 245, Asian Development Bank Institute, September 2010, p. 57. http://www.adbi.org/files/2010.09.02.wp245.national.regional.investors.financing.infrastructure.asia.pdf
32. For a discussion of the evolution of India's "Look East" policy see S.D. Muni, "India's 'Look East' Policy: The Strategic Dimension", *ISIS Working Paper*, Institute of South Asian Studies, Singapore, No. 121, 1 February, 2011. Available at http://www.isas.nus.edu.sg/Attachments/PublisherAttachment/ISAS_Working_Paper_121-_Email-_India's_'Look-East'_Policy_The_Strategic_Dimension_01022011145800.pdf; C Raja Mohan, "Is India an East Asian Power? Explaining New Delhi's Security Politics in the Western Pacific", *ISAS Working Paper*, Institute of South Asian Studies, Singapore, No. 81, 11 August, 2009. Available at http://www.isas.nus.edu.sg/Attachments/PublisherAttachment/ISAS%20Working%20Paper% 2081_21102009212315.pdf. Also see Archana Pandya and David M. Malone, India's Asia Policy: "A Late Look East", *ISAS Special Report*, Institute of South Asian Studies, Singapore, No. 02, 25 August, 2010. Available at http://www.isas.nus.edu.sg/Attachments/PublisherAttachment/

ISAS_Special_ Report_02_-_Email_-_India's_Asia_Policy_-_A_Late_Look_East_26082010093309.pdf

33. See full text of the ASEAN Chairman's statement at the 9th ASEAN-India Summit in Bali, Indonesia, 19 November, 2011. Available at http://www.aseansec.org/documents/19th%20summit/IN-CS.pdf (accessed 35 July 2012)

34. See Shankaran Nambiar, "India's Engagement with ASEAN: Beyond Trade in Goods", ISAS Working Paper, No. 129-26 August 2011, Institute of South Asian Studies, Singapore. Available at http://www.isas.nus.edu.sg/Attachments/PublisherAttachment/ISAS_Working_Paper_129_-_India's_Engagement_26082011163148.pdf

35. Asian Development Bank, "BIMSTEC Transport Infrastructure and Logistics Study", Project Number: 38396, August 2006. Available at http://www2.adb.org/Documents/TARs/REG/38396-REG-TAR.PDF

36. See for instance, C Raja Mohan, "India Eyeing a New Gateway to Southeast Asia", *ISAS Brief*, No. 227-26 January 2012.

37. Pavin Chachavalpongpun, "Dawei Port: Thailand's Megaproject in Burma", *Global Asia*, December, 2011. Available at http://www.globalasia.org/V6N4_Winter_2011/Pavin_Chachavalpongpun.html?PHPSESSID=27e2e5f1eea77f9e245c911358886d55

38. Pavin Chachavalpongpun, "Dawei Port: Thailand's Megaproject in Burma", *Global Asia*, December, 2011. Available at http://www.globalasia.org/V6N4_Winter_2011/Pavin_Chachavalpongpun.html?PHPSESSID=27e2e5f1eea77f9e245c911358886d55

39. *Annual Report* 2004, Ministry of External Affairs, Government of India, p. 8. Also see *The Financial Times*, 9 February, 2004. Available at http://www.financialexpress.com/news/new-delhi-offers-to-study-prospects-of-myanmars-dawei-deep-sea-port/99101

40. *Deccan Herald*, 25 January, 2012.

41. *The Hindu, 25 January, 2012.*

42. *Deccan Herald*, 25 January, 2012.

43. *The Economic Times*, 10 August, 2012.

44. *The Hindu*, 15 October 2011. Available at http://www. thehindubusinessline.com/industry-and-economy/economy/article2537590.ece

45. See Press Release, Gati Ltd., 1 August, 2012, Available at http://www.bseindia.com/xml-data/corpfiling/AttachHis/Gati_Ltd_010812.pdf

46. *The China Post*, 23 July, 2012. Available at http://www.chinapost.com.tw/asia/thailand/2012/07/23/348496/Thailand-pushes.htm

47. For a discussion on the piracy problem in the Strait see Catherine Zara Raymond, "Piracy and Armed Robbery in the Malacca Strait: A Problem

Solved?", *Naval War College Review*, Summer 2009, Vol. 62, No. 3, pp. 31-42. Also see *Voice of America*, 26 September, 2011 and Michael Schuman, "How to Defeat Pirates: Success in the Strait", 22 April, 2009. Available at http://www.time.com/time/world/article/0,8599,1893032,00.html

48. Thant Myint-U, *"Where China Meets India: Burma and the New Crossroads of Asia"*, (New York: Farrar, Straus and Girous: 2011).

49. See for instance Bertil Linter, *Great Game East: India, China and the Struggle for Asia's Most Volatile Frontier*, (New Delhi: HarperCollins, 2012).

50. Arakan Rivers Network, "Preliminary Report on the Kaladan Multi-Modal Transit Transport Project", November 2009. Available at http://www.arakanrivers.net/wp-content/uploads/2009/11/Preliminary-Report-of-Kaladan-Multi-Mulda-Transit-Transport-Project.pdf

51. See *The Myanmar Times,* Volume 31, No. 618, March 12-18, 2012. Available at http://www.mmtimes.com/2012/news/618/news61814.html

52. The term "Constituent Diplomacy" was coined by Professor John Kincaid, a political scientist known for his works on federalism.

53. For a discussion on the Constituent Diplomacy see Ferran Requejo (ed.), *Foreign Policy of Constituents Unites at the Beginning of 21st Century*, (Barcelona: Generalitat de Catalunya, Institut d'Estudis Autonòmics: November 2010); John Kincaid, "Foreign Relations of Sub-national Units: Constituent Diplomacy in Federal Systems", available at http://www.forumfed.org/pubs/StG-Kincaid.pdf

SECTION IV

Defence and Security Cooperation

10
India-Myanmar Defence Cooperation

Vijay Sakhuja

The political transition towards a democratic system in Myanmar has acted as a catalyst and provided an opportunity for India to engage with its neighbour more intimately. In the recent past, there have been several high-level engagements between the political leadership of the two countries; the Indian Prime Minister visited Nay Pyi Taw in April 2012 after a hiatus of nearly 25 years. Both sides exude a new found confidence in their relationship and have agreed to enhance trade to US$ 3.0 billion by 2015.[1] India has promised US$ 500 million line of credit to Myanmar and also agreed to develop livelihood opportunities in border areas and assist in setting up IT infrastructure. Both sides have also agreed to establish network among educational institutions, such as universities and think tanks.

In the defence and security domain, India and Myanmar have acknowledged the need to establish robust security mechanisms for land borders to address the ongoing insurgencies and prevent instability in contiguous areas. In the past, India has supported Myanmar's defence forces through capacity building and has supplied some military hardware. There are plans to train Myanmar military personnel too. As a maritime neighbour, the Myanmar Navy has participated in multilateral maritime forums. These initiatives are significant keeping in mind that India was under enormous pressure to isolate Myanmar at a time when the western world led by the US and several EU countries had imposed a number of sanctions.

In the above context, this chapter attempts to identify the drivers for the bilateral security and defence cooperation and also to understand the geopolitical and geostrategic dynamics that are at play in their relations.

Insurgency in Northeast

One of the important drivers for India to engage with Myanmar is the issue of insurgency in its Northeast. India has a long border with Myanmar, which runs for nearly 1643 kilometres alongside the states of Manipur, Nagaland, Mizoram and Arunachal Pradesh. The ongoing insurgency in the region is not new and has been in existence since the early years of Indian independence. Interestingly, as early as 1950, India had supplied six Dakota aircrafts to Myanmar to fight rebels.[2]

Currently, there are at least eight insurgent or militant groups/ outfits in the area, which have been operating from the Indian and Myanmar territory.[3] It is believed that these groups have received financial, logistic and military support allegedly from external sources in South Asia and also from Southeast Asia. They have established sanctuaries/safe heavens with the connivance of sympathetic groups and communities in the neighbourhood. The Indian security forces have conducted counter insurgency operations, but the insurgents have managed to escape to neighboring areas, where the law enforcement agencies are either weak or disinterested.

However, there have been attempts in the past to flush out these insurgents from Myanmar. For instance, in November 1991, the Myanmar military conducted raids against Manipuri rebel bases and arrested 192 insurgents including UNLF chief Rajkumar Meghen.[4] Apparently, the latter was released by the Myanmar authorities. In 1994, India and Myanmar signed a MoU for the 'maintenance of peace and tranquility in border areas'.[5] This served as a useful instrument to launch Operation Golden Bird in 1995, a joint operation to intercept a huge consignment of arms being transported by insurgent groups from Cox Bazar in Bangladesh to Manipur. The operation came under diplomatic cloud after the military authorities learnt that India had decided to award the 'Nehru Award for International Understanding' to Aung San Suu Kyi.[6]

India and Myanmar have been holding regular border liaison meetings and during the 46th meeting held in August 2012, Myanmar and India discussed several measures along the border aimed at pushing the insurgents out of the Myanmar's territory.[7] India also informed Myanmar that its security forces had stepped up the vigil in the tribal-dominated districts.

Likewise, the Myanmar military initiated 'offensives action in Sagaing Province, against Indian militant camps', but encountered stiff resistance partly due to 'coordination between the insurgents and their affiliates in Myanmar'. In 2012, the attack was successful, but 'all senior leaders in these camps managed to escape unhurt'.[8]

Drug Smuggling

Myanmar has been identified as a major source of poppy cultivation (spread over nearly 43,600 hectares) in Asia and there are several processing units spread in the thick jungles in the north of the country. Although the Myanmar government has taken initiatives to curb poppy cultivation and production, the illicit trade continues.[9] For India, the constants of geography and the location of the two primary sources of illicit opium in Asia, i.e., the Golden Crescent comprising of Afghanistan and Pakistan and the Golden Triangle formed by Myanmar, Thailand and Laos, have resulted in turning it into a transit country for processed narcotics. India has also become a source of precursor chemicals, such as acetic anhydride (AA), ephedrine, and pseudoephedrine, which are used for processing opium.[10]

India and Myanmar have devised a strategy to counter drug smuggling and the issue is discussed at the highest level. Early in 2013, during the annual Home Secretary-level meeting at Nay Pyi Taw, the two sides agreed to initiate necessary steps to prevent the smuggling of drugs, arms and ammunition.[11] In 2010, the two sides had agreed to the Ratification of Mutual Legal Assistance Treaty on Criminal Matters (MLAT) and this legal arrangement is a useful instrument to address a number of transnational crimes including insurgency, drug smuggling and gun running taking place across the borders of the two countries.[12]

Defence Capacity Building

Defence cooperation between India and Myanmar is an important facet of bilateral relations. Both political leaders and military chiefs have visited Myanmar in the past and exchanged views on issues of mutual interest. In January 2013, The Indian Defence Minister visited Myanmar accompanied by a number of senior functionaries of the Indian Ministry of Defence including the Defence Secretary, the General Officer Commander-in-Chief in charge of Indian Eastern Army Command and the Vice Chief of Naval Staff. According to an official press release by the Indian Ministry of Defence, "Both sides [India and Myanmar] will discuss modalities for improving mechanisms for patrolling by their respective forces to curb activities of insurgent groups and other illegal and criminal activities along land and maritime boundaries in their jurisdiction. Both sides also agreed that neither should allow their territory to be used for activities detrimental to the security of the other. Both countries have agreed to conduct periodic coordinated land and maritime patrols."[13]

The Indian Navy appears to have been quite proactive and Indian naval chiefs have visited Myanmar. There have also been regular port calls by Indian naval ships to Myanmar ports. Soon after the visit of the Indian Defence Minister to Myanmar in January 2013, a Myanmar Navy frigate and a corvette made port call at the Indian Navy's Eastern Naval Command Headquarters at Vishakhapatnam in March 2013. The two navies also conducted joint exercises and engaged in coordinated patrol along the maritime boundary between Myanmar's Coco Island and India's Landfall Island, the northern most island of the Andaman group. An official statement by the Indian Defence Ministry noted, "This first-ever such exercise comes soon after [India's] defence minister A.K. Antony visited Myanmar in January to bolster defence ties, ranging from better border management to capacity-building of the Myanmar armed forces."[14]

As far as naval hardware is concerned, in 2006, India announced the transfer of two BN-2 'Defender' Islander maritime surveillance aircrafts and deck-based air-defence guns to the Myanmar Navy.[15] There were plans to help Myanmar establish a naval aviation training centre in Myanmar. It will be pertinent to mention that the decision to supply the aircraft had invited sharp reactions from the UK, which is the original supplier of BN-2 'Defender' Islander to India. The UK had warned that it would stop supply of 'spare parts and maintenance support for them as it opposed the country's military administration.'[16] Further, Myanmar Navy has regularly participated in the Milan meetings held at Port Blair in the Andaman and Nicobar Islands in the Bay of Bengal. During these events, Myanmar is represented either by a senior naval officer or a naval delegation or on occasions by a naval ship.[17]

Military training too has been an agenda of bilateral defence cooperation. In 2006, the Indian Army had offered special warfare training for Myanmar soldiers.[18] In a significant move, during the visit of General Min Aung Hlaing, Commander-in-Chief of Defence Services of Myanmar, to India in August 2012, India once again offered to train Myanmar Army personnel.

As far as other military hardware is concerned, the Indian Army transferred a few light artillery guns and Armoured Personal Carriers (APC).[19] In 2007, there were reports that India had offered the indigenously designed Advanced Light Helicopter (ALH) to Myanmar; but these were denied by the government since the helicopter has a number of EU origin components and any sale would defy the contractual obligations and EU sanctions against Myanmar.[20] Indian Air Force chief during a visit to Nay Pyi Taw in 2006 had offered his Myanmar counterpart generous air force support in upgrading avionics of fighter aircraft in Myanmar's inventory.[21]

Maritime Security

India and Myanmar face a number of maritime security challenges in the Bay of Bengal. These are essentially non-traditional security (NTS) threats, which can emerge in the form of piracy, terrorism, gun running, drug smuggling, illegal fishing, and human smuggling. The Indian Prime Minster also highlighted this issue during his visit to Myanmar in May 2012 and observed that both countries need to expand their security cooperation, which is vital not only to maintain peace along their land borders, but also to protect maritime trade, which he hopes will open up through the sea route between Kolkata and Sittwe.[22] At another level, NTS challenges also include issues relating to climate change and marine environment; and the navies/ maritime forces have been at the forefront to respond to climate change related disasters, providing rescue and relief.

Humanitarian Assistance and Disaster Relief (HADR)

The Bay of Bengal is replete with weather and natural events and the region has been hit by cyclones and Tsunami. In recent times, Myanmar was hit by the 2004 Indian Ocean Tsunami and Cyclone Nargis in 2008, which left 78,000 people dead/missing and affected 2.4 million others.[23] Emergency humanitarian assistance was offered by the navies from a number of countries including the US, Britain and France, but their warships were refused ship-to-shore operations.[24] However, two Indian warships were allowed to enter port to deliver relief materials under Operation Sahayata.[25]

At the operational level, the regional capacity to respond to climate change induced disasters is quite limited. The Indian Navy's capacity to respond to HADR is quite substantive and has been showcased during the 2004 Indian Ocean Tsunami. Since that event, the Indian Navy has acquired a number of naval platforms that are tailored to respond to various HADR mission and roles. However, Myanmar's capability to respond to these challenges is quite low and would require assistance from India.

Oil Infrastructure and Environment Protection

Myanmar is rich in offshore oil and gas reserves and it is estimated that it could be holding nearly 300 bcm of gas. A number of energy companies from China, France, India and South Korea are actively engaged with Myanmar energy companies in exploration activities in nearly 30 offshore oil and gas blocks. These mega offshore energy projects also need to be viewed from the environmental security matrix. In the first half of 2013, Myanmar opened as many as 48 offshore oil and gas exploration blocks and in the future several more blocks will be opened to the oil companies, such as Chevron, BP, Woodside, Royal Dutch Shell, ConocoPhillips, ExxonMobil and Statoil.[26]

Therefore, environmental problems in the form of pollution by enhanced shipping traffic, accidents resulting in oil spills, can have potential impact on the fragile ecosystem in the Bay of Bengal. It is useful to mention that the UN has identified the Bay of Bengal as a Large Marine Ecosystem (LME), which is an environmentally sensitive sea space. Further, these offshore platforms have relatively few security systems and are vulnerable to sabotage. It will be useful to establish 'hot lines' between the maritime enforcement agencies of the two countries to respond to environmental crisis so that requisite response capabilities can be mobilized.

Climate Refugees

The impact of climate change is most noticeable in the Bay of Bengal. There are fears that large tracts of Bangladesh's coastline may be inundated, coastal areas could be contaminated by sea water, which would have adverse impact on agriculture. Such a situation would result in social chaos forcing people to move to other places to seek livelihood. A 2008 report by the National Defence University, Washington concluded that climate change induced events could result in thousands of Bangladeshi refugees entering India. It is plausible that some of these refugees could enter Myanmar illegally through the sea routes. In the past, India maritime security agencies had intercepted a large number of illegal immigrants from Bangladesh and Myanmar, who reached the Andaman and Nicobar coast after they were intercepted by the Thai military and later set adrift.[27]

At another level, there has been a huge exodus by Rohingya Muslims from Myanmar, who are escaping the growing tensions between the Buddhist and Muslim communities in the state of Rakhine since 2012. According to the United Nations, in 2012, nearly 13,000 people fled Myanmar to escape isolation and religious persecution. They have undertaken perilous voyages and as many as

500 may have perished at sea. Nearly 6000 Rohingyas have landed on Thai shores and a large number have been turned away. Some of the rescued Rohingyas have complained of threats, intimidation and inhuman treatment by the Thai authorities, who have denied such allegations. Instead, they have noted that Thailand complies with the established international humanitarian practices and is negotiating with Myanmar and other countries to take the Rohingyas as refugees. In 2009, the Thai security forces were accused of turning away the boat people and some of them were towed out to sea and left to die without adequate supplies. A number of these had arrived on Indian shores in the Andaman and Nicobar Islands. The exodus of Rohingya is not likely to stop and more such boat people can be expected to call on the shores of the neighbouring countries in the coming months. The United Nations High Commissioner for Refugees has urged the regional countries to open their borders to the Rohingyas, who are seeking asylum and international protection and accept them as 'stateless people'.

Geopolitical and Geostrategic Considerations

In recent times, Indian policy makers have begun to position Myanmar prominently in the 'Look East' Policy framework. The Indian Prime Minister has unequivocally stated that Myanmar holds a significant place both in India's Look East Policy and in its collaboration with ASEAN countries under the Initiative for ASEAN Integration (IAI).[28] Besides, Myanmar is an important partner of India in the BIMSTEC and an important node in the Mekong Ganga Cooperation (MGC) initiative.

Myanmar's geographic location serves as a land bridge for India to engage with mainland Southeast Asia. It can facilitate and foster economic growth of India's Northeast region that has remained underdeveloped due to limited connectivity and absence of investments and industrial growth. It is generally agreed that the root cause of the insurgency in India's Northeast has been poor state of socio-economic development in the region resulting in a sense of alienation among the people, who have taken to insurgency. In the above context, the BCIM (Bangladesh, China, India, Myanmar) Cooperation Forum or the Kunming Initiative, a sub-regional grouping, can provide for a Kunming-Mandalay-Dhaka-Kolkata economic zone that can potentially contribute to regional economic integration.[29]

At the strategic level, the tone and tenor of articulations by the Indian strategic community has moved away from labelling Myanmar as a 'satellite of China' and the fears of the Chinese operated electronic surveillance systems in Myanmar appear to have reduced significantly. Apparently, Myanmar had offered to India an access to the often cited surveillance facility at the Coco islands.[30]

However, there are concerns that China's military assistance to Myanmar is continuing and the Myanmar Navy has signed agreement with Pakistan for submarine warfare training[31] clearly suggesting that Myanmar continues to court both China and Pakistan, a relationship that has irked India. It is true that China can offer better military aid package compared to India and, therefore, it is fair to argue that India need not appease the ruling government with military sops; instead, India could explore the possibility of engaging Myanmar in the maritime domain and develop a robust agenda including capacity building to address non-traditional security threats and challenges in the Bay of Bengal. Besides, India is an active participant in the ADMM Plus (ASEAN Defence Ministers Meetings Plus) whose five working groups address NTS issues, thus offering the two partners a substantive agenda for bilateral maritime security cooperation.

It is worth mentioning that Myanmar's parliament announced the nomination of Admiral Nyan Tun as one of the Vice President of the country. It is believed that the Admiral has the reputation as a political moderate[32] and had visited India in 2010.[33]

Concluding Remarks

Myanmar is an important neighbour and it is in New Delhi's interest that a strong and stable Myanmar emerges in the 21st century. There are visible signs of synergy between India and Myanmar to address issues of common concern. Myanmar's assurance to support India in counter insurgency is a reflection of mutual trust and the growing understanding between the two countries. This provides the basis for institutionalized mechanism for sharing intelligence and strengthening of border management systems.

The Bay of Bengal region offers enormous opportunities for greater engagement between India and Myanmar. Among these, cooperation and technological capacity building for HADR operation, search and rescue of fishermen and coordinated patrolling of respective EEZ and responding to illegal migration is critical.

At another level, it remains to be seen how the military establishment in Myanmar responds to India's positive overture. Myanmar is conscious of the rising profile of China and India and these countries naturally appear in its strategic calculus. It would not like a foreign policy predicament, where it has to choose between the two Asian giants. It is cognizant of the Indian naval capability and the military infrastructure being developed in the Andaman and Nicobar Islands and would be apprehensive of offering base facilities to the Chinese Navy turning the otherwise placid and calm waters of the Bay of Bengal into a playground of naval competition. Myanmar can be expected to maintain 'strict neutrality' and engage with both India and China and focus on economic development.

REFERENCES

1. "PM's Address to the Think-tanks, Intellectuals and Business Community in Yangon", *http://pmindia.nic.in/content_print.php?nodeid=1180&nodetype=2* [Accessed on September 2, 2012]. Also see "India, Burma Draw Closer in Military Ties", Mizzima News, August 02, 2012.
2. Nalini Kant Jha and Gaurav Kumar Jha, "India Myanmar Relations: Balancing Morality, Military and Market", *World Focus*, June 2012, p. 55.
3. "Will India-Burma Cooperation Neutralise Northeast Militants?", *The Asian Age*, August 29, 2012. Also see "NE Insurgent Groups Using Myanmar as Safe Sanctuary: Govt.", *DNA*, August 28, 2012. These groups are the Manipur based People's Liberation Army (PLA), United National Liberation Front (ULFA), People's Revolutionary Party of Kangleipak, and Naga insurgent group like NSCN-K and NDFB.

4. Bibhu Prasad Routray, "India-Myanmar Relations: Triumph of Pragmatism", *Jindal Journal of International Affairs*, Volume 1, issue 1, October 2012, p. 315.
5. "'Minimal' Presence of Maoists in Northeast: P Chidambaram", *The Economic Times*, March 21, 2012.
6. Eric Randollph, "Operation Golden Bird and India's Neurotic Relationship with Myanmar". http://www.currentintelligence.net/subcontinental/2011/10/14/operation-golden-bird-indias-neurotic-relationship-with-myan.html [Accessed on September 3, 2012]
7. "46th Indo-Myanmar Border Liaison Meeting", *Manipur Mail*, August 21, 2012.
8. Afsar Karim, "India-Myanmar Cooperation in Combating Terrorism", http://www.bharatdefencekavach.com/News/12653_India-Myanmar-Cooperation-in-Combating-Terrorism.html (accessed on June 28, 2013).
9. Thomas Fuller, "Drug Surge Clouds Myanmar Reform Effort", http://www.livemint.com/2012/05/14205829/Drug-surge-clouds-Myanmar-refo.html [Accessed on August 31, 2012].
10. "No End to Phensidyl Production in Factories Inside India", *The Financial Express* [Dhaka], August 28, 2012.
11. "Yangon Cracks Down on NE Rebel Camps", *The Sangai Express* [Manipur], August 28, 2012.
12. "India Myanmar Home Secretary Level Meeting Concludes Mutual Legal Assistance Treaty on Criminal Matters Ratified", Press Bureau of India, Government of India, December 31,2010.
13. Vivek Raghuvanshi "India, Myanmar Seek Closer Ties With an Eye on China", *Defence News*, http://www.defensenews.com/article/20130122/DEFREG03/301220007/India-Myanmar-Seek-Closer-Ties-an-Eye-China (accessed June 28, 2013).
14. "Myanmar India Launch Joint Naval Exercises", *Mizzima News*, March 11, 2013.
15. Syed Ali Mujtaba "India to Supply More BN2 Aircraft to Burma" *Mizima News*, May 14, 2007.
16. Dipanjan Roy Chaudhury, "India and Myanmar Poised to Boost Ties". [Aaccesed on September 3, 2012]
17. Discussions with retired Indian Navy officers at New Delhi.
18. Brian McCartan "India, Myanmar: Reluctant Brothers in Arms", *Asia Times*, February 19, 2010.
19. "India Burma Relations", http://www.arakanrivers.net/?page_id=147 [Accessed on September 2, 2012]
20. "India rejects Amnesty Report on Copter sale to Myanmar", *The Indian Express*, July 16, 2007.

21. Anil Bhatt, "Will India-Burma Cooperation Neutralise Northeast Militants?", *The Asian Age*, August 29, 2012.
22. "PM's Address to the Think-tanks, Intellectuals and Business Community in Yangon", http://pmindia.nic.in/content_print.php?nodeid=1180&nodetype=2 [Accessed on September 2, 2012]
23. 'Myanmar Tropical Cyclone Nargis', http://www.unep.org/disasters/myanmarcyclone/ [Accessed 28 March 2011].
24. Belanger. J and Horsey. R. 2008. 'Negotiating Humanitarian Access to Cyclone Affected Areas of Myanmar: A Review', http://www.odihpn.org/report.asp?id=2964 [Accessed 30 March 2011].
25. 'Humanitarian Activities and Disaster Relief', http://indiannavy.nic.in/hadr-jul10.pdf [Accessed August 28, 2012].
26. "Myanmar Opens Keenly Awaited Oil Auction", AFP, April 10, 2013.
27. Beckoning of Fortune Traps Rohingyas', The Daily Star [Bangladesh], January 25, 2009.
28. "Joint Statement on the Occasion of the Visit of Prime minister of India Dr. Manmohan Singh to Myanmar", May 28, 2012, Naypyidaw, Myanmar, http://pmindia.nic.in/press-details.php?nodeid=1439 [Accessed on August 27, 2012].
29. Vivek Sengupta, "Strategic importance of Kolkata in Kunming Initiative", South Asia Monitor, Mar 14, 2012.
30. Discussions with retired Indian naval officers.
31. Anthony Davis, "Myanmar Navy starts submarine training in Pakistan", *IHS Jane's Defence Weekly*, June 13, 2013.
32. "Myanmar Names Naval Chief as New Vice President", Associated Press [Naypyidaw], August 15, 2012.
33. "Myanmar Navy Chief Nyan Tun Inspects Guard of Honour Display", ANI, February 22, 2010.

11
Defence and Security Cooperation between Myanmar and India

Aung Myint Oo

Security and regional stability is very important for both Myanmar and India. Myanmar's military is involved in the reform process of Myanmar politics in a key role and it will keep on encouraging the government on its path to democracy and democratic practice. Myanmar views international terrorism, production and proliferation of WMD, gun-running, trans-border crimes, drug trafficking, human trafficking, maritime security threats, natural disasters, deterioration of environment, outbreak of pandemic diseases and illegal migration as non-traditional security threats. To address non-traditional security threats and challenges effectively, India and Myanmar need to enhance bilateral security and defence Cooperation through better transparency, mutual trust and exchange of intelligence and vital information sharing.

Myanmar's defence policy is guided by Myanmar's Constitution. Myanmar's defence policy is mainly based on self defence and non-provocation. Myanmar's defence forces are mainly responsible for safeguarding the Union against any kind of internal dangers and external threats.

Myanmar has been contributing towards the promotion of world peace and stability and has been practicing the Five Principles of Peaceful Coexistence, namely, mutual respect for each other's territorial integrity and sovereignty, mutual non-aggression, non-interference in internal affairs, equality and mutual benefit, and peaceful coexistence, since the establishment of the Non-Aligned Movement (NAM) in 1955 along with NAM's co-founder, India.

Based on these noble principles, Myanmar has never supported any kind of insurgents, tribal armed groups or terrorist groups, who are involved in neighbouring countries, and has never given any safe heaven or sanctuary to them. There were accusations that Myanmar was giving safe heaven or pleasant sanctuary to India's insurgent groups. Such accusations shows that India and Myanmar still need to do a lot more on building mutual trust, exchange information and establishing a closer cooperation in defence and security sectors between the two countries.

The recent incidents that Myanmar has encountered in border regions show that regional stability and security are critical to both countries' political and economic development. Myanmar, shares a long border with its neighbours. It has vast experiences in dealing with border problems, as they can cause huge effects on national solidarity and development in other areas.

Conclusion

If there is peace and stability in the border region, India and Myanmar can promote social and economic development of the people in this regions, which will be beneficial for local people on both sides of the border. Myanmar deeply appreciates India's assistance in the development of Myanmar's infrastructure and in the area of military training. Such kind of assistance will further foster mutual friendship and trust between the two countries. Closer cooperation in defence and security domain will strengthen the relationship between India and Myanmar and further enhance national interests of both the countries. Myanmar looks forward to have more opportunities to promote security and defence cooperation between Myanmar and India.

The Contributors

Dr. Udai Bhanu Singh, Senior Research Associate, Institute for Defence Studies and Analyses, New Delhi, India

U. Kyee Myint, Retired Deputy Director General, Ministry of Foreign Affairs and member of Myanmar Institute of Strategic and International Studies, Yangon, Myanmar

Dr. Vikash Ranjan, Research Fellow, Indian Council of World Affairs, New Delhi, India

Dr. Pankaj Kumar Jha, Research Fellow, Indian Council of World Affairs, New Delhi, India

Dr. Daw Chaw Chaw Sein, Professor and Head of Department of International Relations, Yangon University, Yangon, Myanmar

Dr. Sonu Trivedi, Assistant Professor, Department of Political Science, Zakir Hussain College, Delhi University, New Delhi, India

Dr. Vijay Sakhuja, Director (Research), Indian Council of World Affairs, New Delhi, India

Colonel Aung Myint Oo, Deputy Director, National Defence College, Nay Pyi Taw, Myanmar

Dr. Cho Cho Thein, Professor, Department of Economics, Meikhtila Institute of Economics, Meikhtila, Myanmar

Mr. Sanjay Pulipaka, Fellow, Indian Council for Research in International Economic Relations (ICRIER), New Delhi, India

Dr. K. Yhome, Fellow, Observer Research Foundation, New Delhi, India

Index